C0-AUR-108

IMAGES OF THE URBAN ENVIRONMENT

Images of the Urban Environment

DOUGLAS POCOCK
and
RAY HUDSON

New York Columbia University Press 1978

Published in 1978 in Great Britain by The Macmillan Press Ltd and in the United States of America by Columbia University Press

Printed in Great Britain

Library of Congress Cataloging in Publication Data

Pocock, Douglas Charles David, 1935–
Images of the urban environment.

Bibliography: p.
Includes indexes.
1. Cities and towns. 2. Anthropo-geography.
3. Geographical perception. 4. City planning.
I. Hudson, Raymond, joint author. II. Title.
GF125.P63 1978 301.36 77–14371
ISBN 0–231–04502–6

Contents

List of Figures

List of Tables

Preface

This work has grown out of the authors' joint course in environmental perception given to final-year undergraduates in the Geography Department in Durham. Its focus on the urban environment, broadly interpreted and approached at different scales, is a reflection of the two authors' research interests. Even within this narrowed perspective, however, the treatment of this theme in a short work can be but introductory. Many of the topics mentioned are fields of study in their own right, and the indulgence of the reader is craved for any apparent superficiality in dealing with particular aspects. Numerous references have been deliberately inserted as signposts to the various avenues, while at the same time attempting to steer a straight and coherent path within the totality of this broad, interdisciplinary arena of research and knowledge.

The authors are appreciative of the stimulating environment, physical and social, provided in Durham. They thank Arthur Corner and Paul Wilson for their cartographic efforts, and Edith Pocock for producing a fair typescript from a varied manuscript. Apologies are also due to our families for a somewhat truncated summer.

Acknowledgement is here given to the following persons, bodies and concerns which have kindly agreed to the inclusion of copyright material: the editor and the Royal Dutch Geographic Society for two figures from D.C.D. Pocock (1973). Environmental perception: process and product, *Tijdschrift voor Economische en Sociale Geografie* 64 (in this work figures 3.1 and 3.2); the editor and the Royal Scottish Geographical Society for a figure from D.C.D. Pocock (1972). City of the mind: a review of mental maps in urban areas, *Scottish Geographical Magazine* 88 (figure 5.2); David Canter and Terence Lee for three figures from M. Bateman, D. Burtenshaw and A. Duffett (1974). Environmental perception and migration: a study of perception of residential areas in South Hampshire, *Psychology and the Built Environment* (figure 6.2); Centre for Urban and Regional Studies, University of Birmingham, for figures from B. Goodey (1971). *Perception of the Environment* (figure 7.2) and from

J.R. Gold (1974) *Communicating Images of the Environment* (figure 7.5); the editor and Regional Studies Association for a figure from P.R. Gould and R.R. White (1968). The mental maps of British school leavers, *Regional Studies*, 2 (figure 8.1a); J.B. Goddard for permission to use unpublished results of a survey of residential desirability among teachers (figure 8.1b); Doncaster Metropolitan Borough Council for a figure from their 1971 New Year's card (figure 8.2). Figure 5.1 is based on figures 35 and 36 in *The Image of the City* by Kevin Lynch (1960), by permission of M.I.T. Press, Cambridge, Massachusetts. Figure 5.4 is reprinted from D. Appleyard (1969) 'City designers and the pluralistic city', in *Urban Growth and Regional Development* (L. Rodwin ed.), by permission of M.I.T. Press. Figure 7.1 is taken from figures 5.9–5.12 in *Mental Maps* (1974) by P. Gould and R. White and reprinted by permission of Penguin Books Ltd. Figure 6.1 is based on figure 4 in 'Personal construct theory in the measurement of environmental images' by J. A. Harrison and P. Sarre in *Environment and Behavior*, **7**, no. 1 (March 1975) pp. 3–58 by permission of the Publisher, Sage Publications Inc.

1 Introduction

This work is not about the urban environment *per se* but of man's response to that environment, to the environments of the mind. It is concerned with exploring the subjective manner of construing reality, and with the relevance to personal and social life and behaviour of such mental representations, rather than those of objective reality. Reality is construed differently by different people – and perhaps differently at different times by the same person – a statement readily exemplified at various scales of the urban environment.

The city itself, for instance: is it that which raises man above the level of barbarism, the apex of civilisation, the glorious accumulation of human intelligence, the age-long goal for countless Whittington's, a liberating experience, the place of maximum choice and opportunity of which to tire is to indicate a tiredness with life itself? Or, alternatively, is it a place more akin to hell, a great wen, an anthill of human deprivation and loneliness, a trap, a cosmopolis or necropolis marking the decline of civilisation (Ley, 1974; Schorske, 1966)?

Polar positions, similarly, may be held concerning particular towns. Leeds, for instance, described by Dickens as 'a beastly place, one of the nastiest places I know', was at the same time being described by another author as 'one of the grandest poems which has ever been offered to the world' (Briggs, 1970, p. 79). Again, Chicago struck Kipling as 'inhabited by savages. Its water is the water of Hughli, and its air is dirt . . . I had never seen so many white people together and never such a collection of miserables. There was no colour in the street and no beauty.' In contrast the Better Business Bureau reported that 'In no large city are general living conditions more pleasant than in Chicago . . . a city of miles and miles of streets of quiet homes, flanked by peaceful suburbs' (Strauss, 1968, pp. 41 and 57).

Attitudes towards the suburb are similarly equivocal. Does it represent the successful marriage of town and country, satisfying man's inner craving for nature, providing personal privacy in an unstressful environment? Or is it an uneconomic provision of aesthetic and social sterility (Thorns, 1972)? Again, the city street: to some it is 'an open book, superbly illustrated, thoroughly familiar, yet inexhaustible' (Rudofsky, 1969, p. 21); to others it is a place of unutterable tedium (Harris, 1973). Particular neighbourhoods or buildings similarly evoke different evaluations, not only between individuals or groups of the public but also between the latter and planners. The rise of action groups and preservation societies, and the noise generated at many public inquiries, illustrate this point. The reasons for, and the implications of, such divergent perceptions and attitudes are discussed in the following chapters.

First, the emergence of perception studies within the interdisciplinary field of the behavioural sciences is discussed before turning to an outline of perception, both as process and as product or image. The formidable elicitative problems facing the researcher are then outlined, before exploring the main types of cognitive response, designative and appraisive. Image formation as a learning process is then discussed, before broadening the perspective to conclude with a consideration of the planning and policy implications of image studies.

2 The Emergence of Studies of Environmental Perception and Environmental Images within Geography

The types of study considered in this work are broadly synonomous with that area of geographic enquiry conventionally referred to as environmental perception. As used by geographers, the term perception usually refers to the product of sensory encoding of information, to learned and relatively stable mental conceptions of environments (using this term in a catholic sense, to include social and economic, as well as physical, environments). This usage of the term perception is in contrast to that of psychologists, to whom human geographers have been closely drawn via involvement with studies of environmental images, who more often use the term in relation to the actual sensory process. Learned and stable mental conceptions of environments are referred to as environmental images, mental models of environments, which can be thought of as summarising individuals' environmental knowledge, evaluations and preferences and as having implications for their behaviour. Thus the image may be considered to possess designative, appraisive and prescriptive components, a theme developed in chapter 3.*

It is this multi-dimensional nature of the image, as much as a multi-disciplinary interest in environmental images, that has given rise to

*Images of the environment – like models in general – can be seen as performing a variety of functions. On the one hand, they serve as information storage devices and to classify, categorise, and so differentiate between, and assign meaning to, locations. On the other hand, they serve as a means of explaining, possibly predicting, behaviour.

various and not necessarily synonomous terms to denote the elicited mental model—cognitive map, mental map, spatial schema and perceived environment are but four of the more common examples. Given due cognisance of its make-up, we are satisfied with the generic term 'image'. In fact, related ideas have long been present within geography and can be explicitly traced back to 1913 in the writings of Trowbridge. More generally, though less explicitly, the widespread use of concepts such as 'region' and 'resource' within geography encompasses a broader concern with questions of environmental images. However, it is only in the recent past, say since Lowenthal's important article of 1961, that interest in environmental images has become more widespread within geography.

At this stage, at the outset of the present work, it is appropriate to broaden the scope of enquiry to seek an answer to the question of why, given the long history of closely related ideas within their discipline, should geographers suddenly take on both a more widespread and a more explicit concern with studies of environmental images in a particular period, starting in the early 1960s. To begin to answer this requires a brief and very general review of certain developments in the social sciences in the twentieth century, particularly developments in psychology.

EMERGENCE OF IMAGE STUDIES WITHIN THE SOCIAL SCIENCES

As stated at the outset, an increasing interest in environmental images has led to increasing contact between geographers and psychologists. An understanding of the rise of image studies in geography therefore necessitates a brief consideration of the evolution of modern psychology, in which two broad approaches can be identified—the behaviourist and the cognitive.

Behaviourism, rooted in a tradition going back to Watson (1919) but perhaps most explicitly developed in the stimulus—response theories of Hull (1943; 1951; 1952) and Skinner (1953) is an approach which has no place for 'unobservable' mental concepts such as 'images', denying their scientific validity. Rather attention is focused on such observable and measurable variables as 'behaviour' and the antecedent conditions which precede behaviour. Behaviourism has been particularly important in influencing the path of North

American psychology in the twentieth century.

In contrast, in Europe a variety of approaches with close theoretical affinities to the classical Gestalt theories (Koffka, 1935; Kohler, 1947), which do encompass mental concepts, have been more popular. Of particular interest to geographers concerned with environmental images is the work of Lewin (1935; 1936; 1951) and Tolman (1932; 1948; 1952; 1963) as these contain concepts that are close to those evolved by geographers in relation to environmental images. For example, Tolman (1948) discussed cognitive maps in rats and men, explicitly referring to cognitive representations of spatial environments. Later, Tolman (1952) elaborated his ideas on the mental representations of environments in proposing the concepts of behaviour spaces and belief value matrices. A behaviour space is defined as a psychological space of objects with distance and direction, as perceived by a person at a given moment. Belief value matrices are learned differentiations and categorisations related to objects in the behaviour space. Thus Tolman effectively sees people as possessing mental images of environmental situations, a result of previous learning, which are of central importance in influencing behaviour. Similar ideas are to be found in the writings of Lewin. A central concept in his work is that of life – space, the psychological field of a person that extends from the past, through the present and into the future. Lewin (1951) saw all behaviour as depending to a large degree on the cognitive structure of the life – space.

While the writings of Lewin, Tolman and others of their persuasion abound in such concepts attractive to those interested in studying environmental images, generally there is no explicit specification of ways of operationalising these concepts. Although there are occasional hints, such as Tolman (1952) suggesting the possible use of attitude questionnaires and various projective methods to uncover the content of belief – value matrices, the problem of measurement is generally ignored. This measurement problem proved a serious stumbling block to the development of work on environmental images and its solution had to await advancements in measurement theory and psychometrics (see chapter 4).

It is probably fair to say that since the 1960s there has been a feedback from geographers studying environmental images to the psychologists, reawakening interest in the relationships between people and non-laboratory environments. A new area of environmental psychology has emerged as a distinct sub-discipline, with psychologists showing interest in images of a variety of environments such as rooms, as well as those at spatial scales more familiar to geographers, such as neighbourhoods and urban areas (see Canter, 1975; Craik, 1970). Although as yet somewhat detached from mainstream psychology, there are numerous links between environmental psychologists and geographers studying environmental images.

It is interesting to remember, in relation to the growth of environmental image studies in geography in the 1960s, that in the 1950s there were considerable pressures building up in other social science and design disciplines for more attention to be given to environmental images. There were strong moves within certain quarters of these disciplines towards a concern with peoples' personal and subjective models of environments as the key to understanding their behaviour. So, for example, Katona (1951) argued the need to turn to psychology in order to understand economic behaviour. Boulding (1956), an economist, made a strong, cogent and powerfully argued appeal for the generality of the image as the key, common variable in influencing all behaviour. Simon (1957), whose interests are too wide-ranging to fit neatly into conventional disciplinary boundaries, argued that people construct simplified models of the real world in order that they might successfully chart a course through life's complexities.

At the same time, in certain architectural and planning circles, there was an emerging interest in the impact and meaning of spatial lay-out and design, how people organized and stored information about their built environment, and how they interpreted and made sense of this environment. This interest was most forcefully expressed in Lynch's (1960) seminal work on *The Image of the City*. His study has had considerable impact on the emergent pattern of investigation of environmental images, both methodologically and substantively, in focusing attention on images of urban areas. (The question of image studies and urban and regional policy and planning will be discussed more fully in later chapters.)

Therefore, it is clear that, far from being an isolated movement confined to geography, from the early 1960s the growing interest of geographers in environmental images was rooted more widely and deeply. On the one hand, there was a developing interest in environmental images and individuals' personal worlds as a way of explaining behaviour, an interest that had produced broad cross-disciplinary roots throughout the 1950s. That such an approach was adopted at about the same time in a variety of disciplinary contexts suggests that it is one with considerable explanatory potential. On the other hand, geographers such as Trowbridge (1912) and Kirk (1951) had already explicitly introduced notions of environmental images to the sphere of geography. The profusion of concepts of an essentially cognitive and/or experiential nature present within geography, concepts such as 'region' or 'resource', had implicitly infiltrated similar notions into the discipline. But as was the case in other disciplines, further explicit study and analysis of environmental images in geography awaited progress in available measurement methods (see chapter 4).

IMAGE STUDIES AND RECENT TRENDS IN HUMAN GEOGRAPHY

Here the main concern is with the conceptual, as opposed to the measurement, basis of the recent growth of environmental image studies in geography. It is clear, from previous sections, that historically man–environment relationships have been central to geography and have been an important area in which concepts related to that of the image have flourished and continue to flourish. For example, although not a major concern in this text, there was and continues to be a considerable school primarily concerned with images of environmental risk and hazard, originating in the work of White and carried on subsequently by numerous other researchers. The development of more explicit amd precise ways of tackling environmental images offers great potential in developing such man–environment relationships and has led Wood (1970, p. 129) to claim that:

> The explanation and understanding of a vast range of materials which human geographers study . . . can be greatly increased by consideration of the individual's perception of his environment . . . the study of perception may in time achieve a deep understanding of the man–environment relationship.

This is important not only in stressing the potential value of image studies in understanding man–environment relationships and in restoring these to a central role within geography, but also in pointing out that image studies are potentially applicable to all topics subsumed within human geography. This essentially reiterates Burton's (1963, p. 157) prophetic statement that 'Perception may soon come to merit a place alongside the Quantitative Revolution in terms of significant new viewpoints'. Ignoring for the moment Burton's implication that image studies are non-quantitative, the crucial point to emerge from these two quotations is that studies of environmental images represent the expression of a viewpoint, an approach to and way of conceptualising problems, that is potentially applicable to all areas of study within human geography – man – environment as well as man – man relationships. Such an approach cuts across conventional subdisciplinary boundaries and it is in this context that one must view any study of urban and regional images.

To illustrate the point that image studies do not respect conventional boundaries, it will suffice, for the moment, simply to list some of the topic areas within human geography to which image approaches have been applied, either conceptually or empirically. These are industrial location (Pred, 1967); migration (Wolpert, 1963); urban territoriality (Boal, 1969); environmental hazard evaluation (Saarinen, 1966); retailers' images of their operating environments (Harrison and Sarre, 1975); consumers' images of their retailing environments (Downs, 1970*a*); neighbourhood images (Lee, 1968); city images (Lynch, 1960); regional and national images (Gould and White, 1973). Following the path laid down by Kirk (1951), image approaches have also been adopted in a number of recent studies in urban and regional historical geography. For example, in studies of the images of their new environments held by early explorers and pioneers in Australia (Heathcote, 1965), the North American Great Plains (Lewis, 1962) and the Canadian Prairies (Watson, 1969), a variety of sources were used to recreate these images. It is clear from the diversity of topics cited that many of these studies relate to all or part of the urban or regional environments.

Given the great range of topics within human geography to which image studies have been, or could be, applied, a question arises as to what these diverse studies possess in common that can explain the application of an image approach. A common link can be identified in terms of behaviour: implicity or explicitly, the majority of these various image studies can be traced back to a concern with human behaviour within the range of spatial environments usually recognised as the territory of geographers. The introduction of image approaches into human geography can be usefully considered as one possible approach to understanding spatial behaviour and the processes that influence behaviour. This is useful for two reasons. First, since the 1950s a major concern of many North American and West European human geographers has been the modelling and understanding of spatial behaviour, and, by focusing on behaviour, image approaches can be related to both general changes within geography since the 1940s and to other approaches to understanding behaviour that have been advocated. Second, it is particularly apposite in that a premise (tacit or explicit) of many image studies is that the environmental image underpins behaviour and forms a crucial link mediating between the environment and behaviour in that environment. (For the moment the vexed questions of whether this is a valid premise and whether images change in response to behaviour changing or vice-versa are left undiscussed.) Indeed, in retrospect it seems that attempts to understand behaviour inevitably led to the study of environmental images.

Until comparatively recently, human geography remained dominated by the regional approach and as Berry (1964) has shown, traditional systematic and historical approaches differed from this in emphasis rather than essence. However, disillusionment with the unique, idiographic emphasis of this approach set in, perhaps triggered by Schaefer's (1953) clarion call for geography to become a spatial discipline within the mainstream tradition of physical sciences. While this may be a totally appropriate stance for physical geography, for human geographers it raised some awkward methodological, theoretical and philosophical issues which at the time were not perceived.

From the late 1950s the floodgates opened and, aided by the increasing availability of the computer, a fresh tide of conceptual and methodological changes swept through geography, identified by the catch-phrase 'Quantitative Revolution'. Emphasis switched from description of the unique to explanation and/or prediction (a positivist approach would see the two as synonomous) of more general classes of events, using a variety of mathematical and statistical modelling approaches.

A basic problem that rapidly emerged was the absence within geography of adequate theories to explain regularities uncovered by such quantitative analyses. It is one thing to describe a relationship, for example a relationship between numbers of migrants and distance between origin and destination, by some neat mathematical or statistical function, something rather different to satisfactorily explain this in terms of underlying process. Given this situation, two avenues were open to geographers and regional scientists: either invent indigenous spatial theories or adopt theories from other disciplines, a process that was already underway by this time. Whether the former option is feasible remains a moot point; what is undeniable is that geography has overwhelmingly tapped other disciplines in search of theory (Harvey, 1967).

Type of Analysis	Level of Analysis	
	Aggregate	Individual
Normative		
Non-normative		Behavioural Cognitive

Figure 2.1 Typology of approaches to the study of spatial behaviour within human geography (Source: Hudson, 1974*a*)

The variety of adopted approaches to theories and explanations of behaviour in human geography can be conveniently summarised as a simple matrix, based on two classificatory criteria (figure 2.1). Normative studies, prescribing optimal patterns of spatial behaviour in relation to given objectives, can be distinguished from non-normative, or, to borrow a distinction from economics, positive studies aimed at explaining or understanding actual behavioural patterns. Again, one may examine either the behaviour of individual units (persons, firms) or aggregates of these. A notable omission from this classification scheme is the time dimension. While there are exceptions that are explicitly concerned with the explanation of temporal change in spatial patterns (for example, diffusion studies), generally the dominant approach to theory in human geography has been ahistorical, static and cross-sectional. Various approaches have been stressed at different times and in different places, but broadly their introduction into human geography proceeds from the top left to the bottom right hand cell of the matrix. A few words on each of these methods will help to explain the emergence of environmental image studies as a means to understand spatial behaviour.

Normative, aggregate attempts to explain spatial structure and behaviour, such as those of Isard (1956) and Lösch (1954) which are concerned with locational patterns of economic activity, are based on a tradition extending back through the work of Christaller and Weber to that of von Thunen in 1825. Such approaches draw heavily though not exclusively on a well-developed corpus of deductive micro-economic theory: the neoclassical theory of the firm. The prime emphasis of these approaches is on the equilibrium conditions of various sectors of the locational – economic system. Individual decision processes and behaviour are handled via a set of assumptions of the individuals' knowledge and motivations, generally personified as Economic Man. All actors of a given type are assumed identical, each with complete and perfect knowledge; all entrepreneurs have the same aim, say to maximise profits or minimise production costs; all consumers aim to minimise their movement costs, subject to satisfying their needs. Put another way, all actors of a given type are assumed to have identical and – in relation to their assumed goals – comprehensive environmental images.

While of some use in offering certain, if limited, insights into the conditions necessary for various sectors of the space – economy to attain a state of static partial equilibrium, such approaches are of little use in explaining why people behave as they do. The social and psychological determinants of behaviour are merely assumed. It is noteworthy, as pointed out above, that in the 1950s a number of prominent economists were indicating the need to probe beneath the behavioural assumptions of neoclassical economics at a time when geographers and regional scientists were increasingly attracted to theories of spatial economic structure, erected on the basis of an uncritical acceptance of such behavioural assumptions. Indeed, these behavioural assumptions are a necessary condition for the derivation of equilibrium spatial structures. Moreover, they become untenable in a spatial context. In particular, because of the costs of information acquisition (see chapter 7), perfect knowledge – and so the remaining assumptions – become untenable (Pred, 1967). However, the unreality of these behavioural assumptions was not without important consequences. First, at the level of the individual, it focused attention on the actual determinants of choice. Second, it generated efforts to produce descriptively more accurate models of aggregate behaviour.

Before going on to discuss these alternative approaches to behaviour, normative studies of individual behaviour may be briefly mentioned and quickly dismissed as there are close links between the theoretical background of these and that of the aggregate approaches just discussed. The objective of such an approach is to specify optimal behaviour patterns for individuals, given assumptions as to their goals, level and amount of knowledge and so on. The two most common variants of this approach are linear programming, concerned with optimisation under conditions of certainty (see Cox, 1966), and game theory, concerned with optimisation under conditions of uncertainty (see Gould, 1965; Stevens, 1961). The behavioural assumptions of linear programming and game theory formulations are open to broadly the same criticisms as those of normative location theories.

Non-normative, aggregate studies are perhaps best exemplified by reference to the gravity model and related spatial interaction models (see Wilson, 1971). If normative approaches have relied primarily on neo-classical economics for their theoretical bases, these non-normative approaches, to the extent that they do have a theoretical basis, rely on probability theory. Essentially, the behaviour of human social systems is held to be analogous to that of physical systems (a criticism that can also be levelled at the conceptualisations of social systems contained in neo-classical economics). Similarly, the behaviour of individual people is held to be analogous to that of individual molecules: that is, individual choice is treated as the outcome of a stochastic (or random) process.

The seeds of the gravity model as a model of spatial behaviour were sown early; for example, in the work of Ravenstein (1885) on migration and in that of Reilly (1931) on consumer behaviour. Originally based on an analogy with Newtonian mechanics, most explicitly developed by Stewart (1950) in terms of 'social physics', the gravity model has subsequently been much criticised because of this and the resultant absence of an adequate theoretical basis (for example, by Isard, 1960). To some extent such criticisms have been answered by Wilson (1971), who, using entropy maximising methods, shows the gravity model to be but one of a family of related spatial interaction models.

An entropy maximising approach draws on analogies with statistical rather than Newtonian mechanics. Individual choice is explicitly treated and conceptualised as the outcome of a random process, subject to certain over-all constraints. As such, nothing is revealed of the individual decision processes underlying individual behaviour –

the approach being explicitly designed to treat this as the outcome of a random process. Indeed, it is reasonable to suggest that such approaches reveal more about the spatial structure of the environment, via the various constraints placed on behaviour in aggregate, than about individual choice processes. It has been argued that if studies of aggregate movement patterns can be linked to studies of individuals' knowledge and motives, explanatory inferences may become possible (Olsson and Gale, 1968). However, initial attempts suggest that the forging of such links may not be feasible (Hudson, 1976*a*).

Thus, having briefly explored a variety of approaches to spatial structure and behaviour, a consistent pattern has emerged in that each of these makes assumptions as to peoples' knowledge and aims rather than directly investigating them. Having explored these various approaches, one is left with having to confront individual behaviour and its determinant processes directly.

Two types of non-normative study of the individual can be distinguished: that concerned with individual behaviour *per se*, and that concerned with the processes that underpin individual behaviour. In the former, attention is focused on behaviour in an attempt to infer the underlying processes from the observed behaviour. However, the chief interest in studies adopting such an approach is usually less with individual decision processes than with the socio-spatial constraints that shape behaviour. A good example of this type of study is time – space budget analysis (Anderson, 1971). The alternative is to study decision processes directly. In practice this usually proves to be a study of environmental images, these being taken as a surrogate for the decision process. Thus attention is directed towards individuals' environmental knowledge, preferences and evaluations, in the belief that these underpin behaviour; in this context, studies of the appraisive aspects of images, emphasising meaning, are more likely to prove useful in explaining behaviour than those of the designative aspects of images.

Numerous conceptual schema have been proposed linking up environmental images, learning, sources of knowledge and behaviour (for example, Downs, 1970*b*). But empirical studies of the links between images and behaviour are rare. Such links are usually left as an implicit assumption rather than being explicitly developed; as yet most studies of environmental images have concentrated on the designative and appraisive functions of the image.

THE WIDER IMPACT OF ENVIRONMENTAL IMAGE STUDIES WITHIN GEOGRAPHY

We have said that the call made by Schaefer in 1953 for geography to become a spatial discipline in the mainstream tradition of physical science had momentous implications for human geography. The adoption of physical science philosophies and methods, either directly or indirectly, by human geographers inevitably, if perhaps unintentionally, led to the concept of social systems as analogous to physical systems (as, for example, in partial equilibrium location theories and gravity model approaches to spatial interaction). In essence, such analogies denied the fundamental point that social systems are dynamic and made up of people as opposed to particles. At the same time the focus of interest shifted both from geography's traditional concern with man – environment relationships and analyses of actual patterns of man – man relationships to a more arid concern with abstract analyses of spatial systems *per se*.

As stressed above, studies of environmental images represent the expression of a viewpoint – a way of looking at problems that both arose, in part, as a reaction to the mechanistic views of behaviour implicit within location theory and spatial systems approaches and subsequently acted to check these trends. The emergence of image studies has led to a refocusing of interests within geography, both in terms of questions asked and in the methods chosen to investigate the questions raised. The various strands may be summarised. First, image studies have led to a much greater focus on the individual *per se*, who is now treated more as a 'white' rather than a 'black box'. Second, there has been a greater focusing on man – environment relationships, offering a possible way of ending the human – physical dichotomy other than in terms of common spatial techniques, and a different perspective on man – man relationships. Third, a possible way has emerged of reinterpreting much regional geography in terms of an expression of various authors' images of regions, while, as noted above, image approaches have become quite widely used in studies in historical geography, again fusing old and new concerns in the discipline. Over all it has ushered in a generally more humane attitude, perhaps opening the door to an altogether more mature approach to theory within human geography (Harvey, 1973).

This refocusing of interest is not without methodological and philosophical implications. The quantitative revolution and all that it entailed was based on a methodology developed in the context of the physical sciences and brought with it, seemingly by the back door and unwittingly, the associated philosophical position of positivism (Harvey, 1969*a*). Positivism may be characterised by an adherence to empirical truth and logical consistency (Walmsley, 1974). That there are certain limitations inherent in this approach to problem definition and solution has long been recognised by physical scientists, both in the context of their own work (Bridgman, 1959) and in the context of applying methods developed in the physical sciences to human problems (for example, see Oppenheim, 1956).

Recently, and following in the trail blazed by Lowenthal (1961), certain human geographers such as Harris (1971), Guelke (1971) and Harvey (1973) have taken up this latter theme. As a result, there is a substantial and vocal minority of human geographers who call for the rejection of positivist methods and philosophy on the grounds that these are totally inappropriate for dealing with human problems. This call is based on the recognition that there are a multitude of paths to knowledge, a multitude of beliefs as to what constitutes the truth. In turn, this recognition reflects the growth of image studies and the explicit recognition that different people see the 'same' environmental situation in different ways.

However, no single non-positivist philosophy has arisen to displace positivism, although several have been advocated (see Harvey, 1973; Mercer and Powell, 1972). Prominent among these has been phenomenology (see Lowenthal, 1961; Relph, 1970; Tuan, 1971*a*), but, like other potential rivals to positivism, this has its own set of problems.

Rather than replace positivism, the main impact of considering these other possible positions within geography has been a change in the prevalent type of positivism, although whether this can be more than a short-term accommodation is open to serious doubt (see Lewis and Melville, 1976). Positivism has persisted partly due to the depth of its own entrenchment, partly because of the problems besetting rival positions. This transformed version one may refer to as neopositivism. Adoption of this neopositivist position implies a recognition that current theories and modes of thought influence empirical observation and the delimitation of the bounds of permissible subject matter. Put another way, it is a viewpoint that questions '. . . the degree to which science can be objective' (Olsson, 1970).

Thus, it represents a compromise position, an explicitly value-conscious positivism, aiming at an objective treatment of subjectivity (and vice versa). As such, it is important to an appreciation of studies of environmental images (see chapter 4) while at the same time owing its rise within geography to the increasing popularity of such studies.

A SUMMARY OF THE CURRENT STATE OF THE ART

There are several points that can be made to summarise this deliberately wide-ranging introductory chapter which are of relevance to what follows. The first is that most studies of environmental images have been carried out on an urban or intra-urban scale. There has been much less work in non-urban contexts or on units of a larger scale than the urban area – hence the emphasis here on urban images, although regional images are by no means ignored in later chapters.

A second point is that the image is conceived as possessing a multidimensional character, having designative, appraisive and prescriptive aspects. The nature of the image is more fully explored in the next chapter, and studies of the designative and appraisive aspects of the image in chapters 5 and 6.

A third point is that, to date, studies have generally concentrated on measuring the structure and content of the image. The relation of images to behaviour has usually been left implicit rather than made explicit. Such concentration on these aspects reflects the considerable conceptual and mensural problems posed by an approach centred on consideration of environmental images, which it was necessary to overcome to allow the fruitful maturation of this approach (Harvey, 1969*b*). Chapter 4 is given over to consideration of these problems and proposed solutions to them.

A related point is that many of these studies represent a rather curious mixture of individual and group components. While frequently results are presented in terms of group images, measurement of images is carried out at the level of the individual, often in an *ad hoc* and atheoretical manner. Such an approach also typifies the aggregation from individual to corporate group images.

A corollary of the last two points is that there has been a relative neglect of process, of the learning that gives rise to environmental images, both at a conceptual and empirical level. The latter reflects problems of data collection. The former results from a failure to view image studies in the context of their wider social structural setting of differential access to knowledge and information. However, questions of learning are increasingly being considered by those interested in environmental images and are taken up in chapter 7.

Finally, environmental image studies, in common with many other areas of concern to human geographers, have increasingly been considered in terms of their practical and policy implications (Goodey, 1974*b*). Environmental psychologists have shown a similar increasing interest in the policy relevance of their work (for example, Stringer, 1975). This aspect is developed in chapters 8 and 9. Exploration of these various themes enumerated above begins with a more detailed discussion of the nature of environmental perception and the image.

3 The Nature of Environmental Perception and the Image

After discussion of the emergence of image studies in geography, attention is here turned to consider more specifically the nature – the what, why and how – of environmental perception. Illustrations are taken from the urban environment, where the meso-scale is the most common level of investigation, but much of the discussion is applicable to a variety of contexts and varying degrees of resolution. The process of environmental perception and image formation is presented first before turning to the product or characteristics of the image so formed.

DEFINITIONS AND BACKGROUND

The term perception is a broad one embodying a multitude of definitions and meanings, whether referring to the actual process of perceiving or to the end product of that process. Often the definition is implied rather than explicit; some decry any over-emphasis on definitional precision (Warr and Knapper, 1968, pp. 2–4). Saarinen (1969, p. 5) notes that the *International Encyclopaedia of the Social Sciences* takes over fifty pages to discuss the meaning of perception. Here we may narrow the focus to social perception – rather than to its neurological and physical aspects – concerned with the cognitive structuring of social stimuli (physical, and associated social, environment) as influenced by the perceiver's genetic structure and cultural characteristics.

In the classical and strict sense perception relates to situations where stimulus is present (Ittelson, 1973, pp. 1 – 19), being a middle step in a hierarchical process of sensory awareness between sensation, which is the initial, unorganised response to a stimulus, and cognition, which represents a general awareness, a summary of all previous stimuli, none of which needs actually be present. Awareness or interaction with the environment is achieved primarily by the visual sense experience, although it is clearly an amalgam with auditory, olfactory and tactile sensations. In the present context, however, perception refers to more than direct apprehension by the senses – the product of which may be termed percepts – for the perceived environment or image is more than the sum of direct perceptual experiences. Perception is therefore used neither in a physical nor in a strictly literal sense, but more extensively – akin to cognition, awareness or, even, understanding. Such a definition, incidentally, is consistent with the Latin origin, 'percipere', to comprehend (Goodey, 1971, pp. 2–3). The image is thus the sum of direct sensory interaction as interpreted through the observer's value system, and accommodated in the existing memory store where inputs from indirect sources may be of at least equal importance. Often it may also relate to spaces more extensive than can be apprehended in the narrow, perceptual sense.

Turning from perception to the adjectival prefix, environment is taken to refer to anything external to the perceiver which influences, or might influence, the perception process. The basic dimensions of the 'environmental display' to which man responds have been discussed recently by Craik (1968), who is the author of this apposite term. The focus in image studies, therefore, is wider than that which is characteristic of works in urban morphology, the built environment or townscape, where the physical component is exclusively or overwhelmingly emphasised.

The most obvious, and at the same time the most fundamental, point to emerge from the above definition is the interdisciplinary nature of the field. Environmental perception is a term for one of a series of different approaches which are contributing an increasing corpus of knowledge at the boundary zone of disciplines as traditionally conceived. The geographer, concerned with man – land relationships, clearly has an obvious interest in this area of convergence or overlap.

The present work does not attempt to explore the theoretical underpinning of this new zone of interest, but clearly its foundations lie rooted in philosophy, the subject traditionally concerned in speculating about the ultimate nature or meaning of things. Aesthetics, whether seen as distinct from philosophy or not, contains the poles of personal interpretation and universality, while psychology with its concern with the mind of man is of special relevance. The rise of environmental psychology has highlighted this relevance and also the special relationship of that discipline to those geographers with an awakened interest in the subjective, as opposed to objective, environment.

Given a common interest by both geographers and psychologists in man – environment relationships, and in view of increasing interdisciplinary team work in which concepts and techniques may be shared, any distinctive geographical viewpoint may seem irrelevant. Intrinsically, however, the geographer is involved in the man – environment relationship in order to better understand man's use of, or behaviour in, the environment. The psychologist, on the other hand, studies the field from the point of view of man and his psychological processes in order to explain how the environment is known. As a result there is a different interpretation put upon the concept of the image. To the geographer the image is a filter between man and the environment. Taking a strong positivist view of knowledge and reality, he seeks to elicit this image and to compare its isomorphism to the objective or real world, often by means of mapping. To the psychologist, on the other hand, the objective environment is 'unknowable', being a personal construction. In the words of Neisser, 'we have no direct, *im*mediate access to the world, nor to any of its properties . . . Whatever we know about reality has been *mediated*' (Neisser, 1967, p. 3).

In terms of research topic a further distinction is evident on the basis of scale. The geographer, even during the behavioural era, has remained largely wedded to the meso-scale. The psychologist, even when he abandons unreal or rodent environments, works characteristically with small spaces – with personal behaviour in lifts, in rooms, at the table and inside institutions.

The purpose – the why – of perception and image formation may be answered in terms of a healthy and comfortable existence. The former concerns the compromise between the finite capacity of the human brain and the infinite complexity of reality. The brain is genetically limited – to processing seven pieces of information at any one time or to recording up to eighteen impressions – and is thus forced to select from the wealth of potential sensory information.

Without this filter the condition of information overload would result in confusion and mental unbalance. The second reason, comfort, subsumes the conditions of security, orientation, ease of movement and pleasure. Familiarity holds the key. Recollect, for instance, the feeling of unease which accompanies one's initial encounter with a large city. Lack of knowledge of where one 'is at' felt on emergence from a pedestrian subway or underground station, or when driving a car in a busy, strange city, can induce a state of considerable confusion. Alternatively, a rapid disappearance of familiar buildings and landmarks can induce a feeling of bewilderment or 'future shock' (Toffler, 1970). An extreme example of environmental dissonance – ignoring experiments at solo, subterranean survival – is provided by the bewilderment experienced by newly-released prisoners (Sommer, 1969, p 95).

The process – the how – of perception is a mental filtering, coding, storing and retrieving through the joint functioning of the limbic system along with the two parts of the neocortex or higher brain. From the point of view of social, rather than neurological, perception the process may be conceptualised as a complex interactive one between man and the environment. The component parts of this process and the resultant environmental image are summarised in figure 3.1, which is an expanded version of a conceptual model originally designed for person perception (Warr and Knapper, 1968). It presents as a single snapshot what is in fact a continuous cycle, a series which may be considered as constituting the learning process.

MODEL OF ENVIRONMENTAL PERCEPTION

The conceptual model shows a threefold set of stimuli forming the input, relating to the characteristics of, previous information on and present context within which the environment is being perceived. That part of the information store relating specifically to a particular stimulus and derived from past stimulus – response situations of the same environment is considered sufficiently distinctive from the total memory store to constitute a separate entry at the input stage. Certainly past experience, whether first-hand or from secondary sources, is crucial to the attitude adopted towards, and the interpretation of, an existing scence. This is illustrated in a novel manner in Turner's painting of Venice in which his debt to the past is

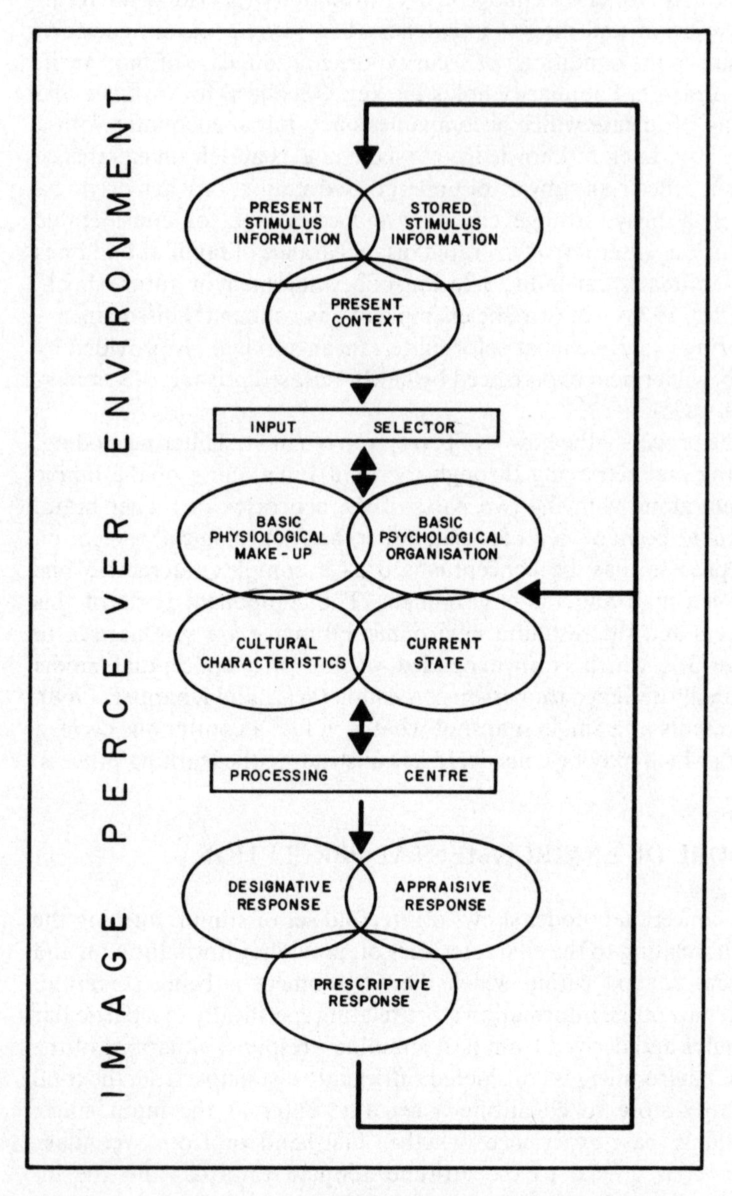

Figure 3.1 A conceptual model of environmental perception for image studies (Source: Pocock, 1973, p. 252)

expressed by the insertion of a small figure of Canaletto, complete with easel. In Boulding's words (1956, p. 174), 'part of the image is the history of the image'.

Present context refers to the spatial context or setting: the platform from which the environment is perceived. Two basic dimensions are the degree of contact or involvement and the degree of movement. The contrast brought by differences of involvement can be seen by comparing perception from inside a vehicle, with its loss of detail, awareness and appreciation only of visual changes, with that of a pedestrian, open to the full range of sensory perception. Ground angle and texture, street sounds and smells and changes in micro-climate are all monitored in the richer experience of the pedestrian context.

Williams has summarised five different categories of perception based on various ways in which the city can be observed – panorama, skyline, vista, urban open space and experience in motion (Williams, 1954). Any deep or balanced appreciation, however, is an accumulation of a variety of contexts knitted together in a sequential experience. Thiel's suggestion that architecture may be considered 'frozen music', like a phonograph record with man 'the pickup whose movement realises the experience' (Thiel, 1962, p. 33), is but one analogy to the city being a work of art. Others liken it to a poem or to a language to be read. The unifying element is that appreciation is dependent on time and movement with the consequent accumulation of experience.

The effect of movement while perceiving the environment, memorably captured by Wordsworth in *The Prelude* where the lone night rower panics at the growing skyline silhouette above the lake, can be readily appreciated in any city with some distinctive landmark. In Durham, for instance, the remark of the tourist that from one part of the city the prominently sited cathedral looked like the QE2, while from another like Apollo 13 on its launching pad, is a colourful acknowledgement of this phenomenon. Moreover, it is not only differences in angle of vision, but also the order and sequence in which the environment is experienced that have an influence on the image formed. This is emphasised in townscape studies, where certain aesthetic experiences or appreciations require that a particular progression be followed (Cullen, 1961; Sharp, 1968). Two further points of relevance here are the disproportionate influence on the image of the first encounter with a place – an event which can never be repeated – and the law of diminishing returns which sets in after several encounters with the same place when, technically, fixation has superseded the earlier perceptual processes of selection, accentuation and interpretation. At this stage we see in effect what we want to see, having turned a blind eye to much that is present. Only a change of involvement or a period of absence followed by a revisit can reactivate a heightened perception of the same scene. This general process is illustrated in Gans' study of the working-class district of Boston known as the West End. His initial perception was one of contrast between attraction and delapidation, but with increasing involvement in a study of the inhabitants the empty tenements and stores slipped from his image (Gans, 1962).

Turning to the individual, perceiving is considered to take place in a 'tuned' organism already 'to some extent *prepared* for seeing, hearing, smelling, tasting' (Bruner, 1951, pp. 123–4). The process is thus one of categorisation, of developing generalised concepts, built up from a hypothesis-forming and testing attitude to the environment. The alternative to this inquisitive attitude is what Popper has called the bucket theory, with the mind an empty receptacle for impressions from the environment (Popper, 1972).The actual choice of, and response to, stimuli may be conceptualised as the interaction between four components, two of which are inherent or mechanical in nature, the other two being cultural or interpretive in origin.

The basic physiological make-up would seem to need little elaboration. Only a small minority have (unadjusted) inherent sensory disability. For these, reliance on one particular sense produces not simply a heightened response in that dimension, but an image which has to be 'relearnt' and harmonised should the sense disability be rectified. This has been shown by research among people whose sight has been restored (Gibson, 1950, pp. 216–20). Within these self-evident categories, however, lies a vast range of degrees of responsiveness to sensory stimuli. It is well-known that some have a 'sharp' nose, others acute hearing or taste, while sensitivity to changes of temperature, humidity, noise or pain quite manifestly varies from person to person (Tuan, 1974*a*, pp. 5–12). Each individual is unique in his genetic make-up, and thus in sensitivity, temperament and personality. Degrees of sensitivity to the environment are therefore to be expected quite apart from any accentuation or diminution in sensory activity stemming from social – cultural background. As a result, one author has suggested the concept of an environmental personality, distinct from although analagous to social personality, and defined as the predisposition to behaviour in the non-interacting geographical environment (Sonnenfeld, 1969).

Vision is the dominant sensory mode and contributor to the image, such that the phrase 'seeing is believing' implies that mere sight is proof, while the word 'see' is commonly used to mean 'understand'. The dominance of the eye may be readily tested in any city park, where a closing of one's eyes will immediately release much of the urban cacophony previously screened by the vision-dominated scene in which not only the greenery *per se* but also the evocative association of nature's tranquillity, have shaped the over-all response. Even on city streets it is possible for visual variety to override traffic noise, to the extent that a street with frequent car horns sounding may be deemed 'quiet' (Lynch and Rivkin, 1959, p. 29).

A second inherent characteristic of universal relevance is the psychological element which provides the underlying organisational principles through man's apparent tendency to perceive form and shape in modified form. The Gestalt explanation for this is that psychological organisation is always as 'good' as prevailing conditions allow (Koffka, 1935, p. 110). In general 'our impressions are not psychologically equivalent for all positions . . . stages between the major ones have the character of indefiniteness about them and are readily seen in the sense of one or the other adjacent Prägnanzstufen or major stages' (Wertheimer, 1938, p. 79). In addition to the figure – ground relationship, the literature contains over a hundred laws of Gestalten explaining how the objective arrangement dictates what is seen, bringing a spontaneous grouping and differentiation to produce good or meaningful structure. Of the total, some half dozen laws or principles are of general significance – those of proximity, similarity, closure, common fate, common movement and experience.

An alternative explanation of the tendency to inherent modification is a perceptual economising in which the eye and brain, following the principle of 'near enough is good enough', registers just sufficient for recognition and classification and ignores the remaining, 'redundant' detail (Attneave, 1954, pp. 183 – 93). Whatever the cause, there is a perceptual tendency to register simplicity, clearness and order rather than the haphazard. The mental image therefore mirrors a greater degree of 'goodness' than is actually possessed by the real world. Moreover, since it seems logical to assume that a similar process continues to operate on the memory store, it has been deduced that the residue of earlier stimulations becomes increasingly simple and ordered. This 'changing trace' hypothesis is only partially proven, however, for some changes which occur in the memory clearly result in a less complete or poorer figure.

The organisational tendency, demonstrated in psychology texts by point and line diagrams, is most apparent from mental map exercises, where general symmetry and regularity are prominent. Figure 3.2 shows the results of an exercise conducted with second-year geography undergraduates, a sample population familiar with the areas concerned and for whom the mapping technique should present no problems. The top row of figure 3.2 shows the exercise as presented, with the additional information that the frames ran north – south and east – west. Charley's Cross is adjacent to the university science site, with the Geography building the nearest one to the road intersection; Claypath is one of the three roads leading from the central Market Place; Crossgate leads to the main road to the west. The instructions were to insert the particular streets. The results strongly confirm the hypothesis: intersections are seen as right angles, the cumulative effect of small curves is ignored, and cardinal points exert undue influence. Other exercises have shown similar results (for example, de Jonge, 1962). Perhaps the best known is the so-called 'Boston Common phenomenon' (Stea, 1969*b*, pp. 72–3), the Common forming a five-sided figure but often 'simplified' into four by strangers who consequently find themselves out of phase with the environment.

The tendency to schematic simplification in the perception and recollection of spatial relationships has recently prompted an attempt to produce detailed perceptual maps of selected British cities to compare their efficacy with the conventional map or street-plan (Fisher, 1972, 1973). It probably explains the success of simple 'orientation maps' issued by various transport and tourist agencies. The best known example is the map of the London underground system. Little wonder, then, before the advent of navigational and surveying techniques, when the logicality of the mind was reinforced with belief in divine order, that maps should contain a high degree of symmetry.

Perception, however, is more than a mechanical process, passively recording the physical properties of stimuli through some inborn organising action of the nervous system. From the general nativism –

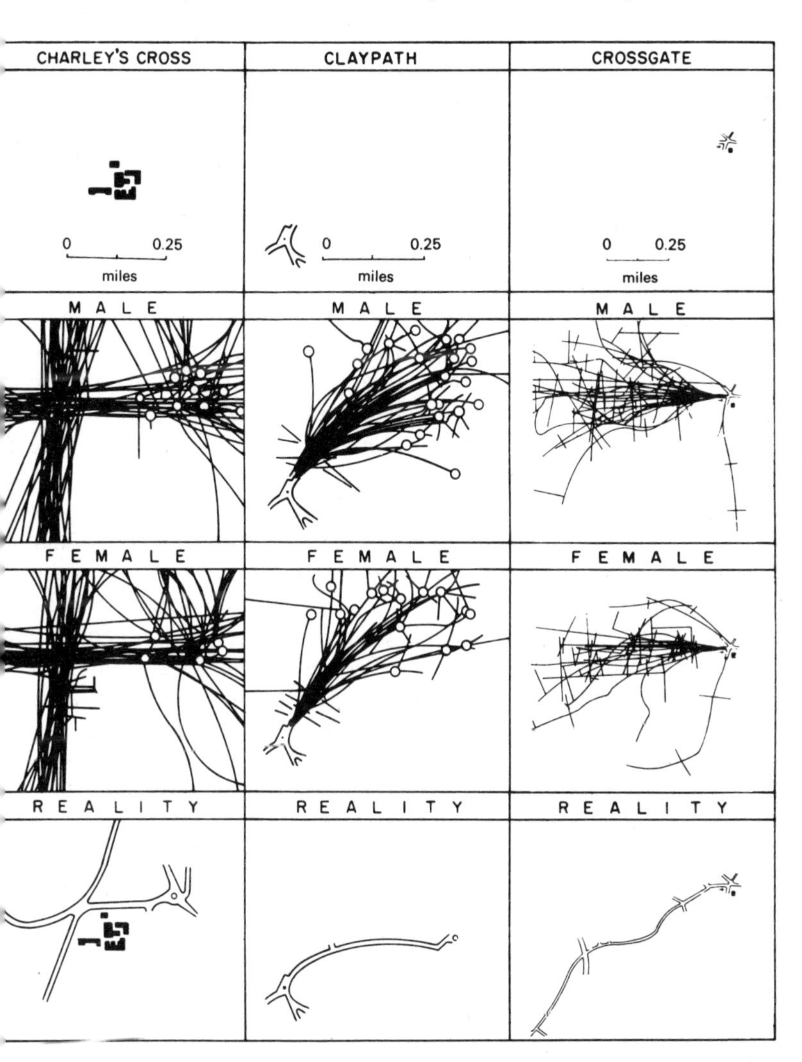

Figure 3.2 Mental maps and reality: good figure tendency shown in student exercise, Durham, 1972 (Source: Pocock, 1973, p. 254)

empiricism debate, it is evident that the registered image is as much a concern of the mind as of the brain: of things experienced and learnt as of things given. Perception is thus an active process of interaction between the perceiver and the environment in which differences in physical, functional or emotional significance of the latter lead to highly personal responses. A deliberate, culturally-induced choice or selection from the total stimuli is made. Two cultural or interpretive components are postulated at the perceiving stage, distinguished according to whether the selection relates to enduring or momentary conditions.

The stable cultural characteristics producing a personal response include the individual's personality attributes, attitudes, social class, age, sex and so on. Of these, attitudes is perhaps the most important element conditioning perception. This is evident if attitude is interpreted as the summary of past experiences or perceptions. Composed of a collection of feelings and beliefs, including evaluative beliefs, an attitude disposes an individual to behave or perceive new situations in a particular way. Thus nothing is approached in a state of innocence.

Critical to the mediation of sensory information is the prevailing cultural milieu, both of the broad society and of particular subgroup(s) within that society into which the individual is born, spends what is termed his 'formative years', and with which he subsequently associates. Within any society the receiving, acceptance and reinforcement of information is inextricably bound up with group membership so that an individual's value system and attitudes tend to reflect those of the group norm (for example, Bulmer, 1975). In brief, the prevailing cultural milieu 'coerces the individual into conformity . . . so that with rare exceptions, he can think, act, believe, and aspire only in accordance with the dictates of his culture' (Frank, 1948, p. 171). Recognised townscape or building 'styles' or 'tastes' are thus societal filters through which places are seen and assessed. A classic example of this is the evaluation of landscape in the eighteenth century when painters and writers developed a highly formal style of representation that influenced not only the period's landscape gardeners but also the way in which the literate public would view any scene, such that topographic variation and actual detail were subjugated to suggestion of, and approach to, the ideal conception (Barrell, 1972).

Places, then, are seen through acquired cultural filters of standards, expectations, and so on, an approach tantamount to 'believing is seeing' rather than the reverse, 'seeing is believing', mentioned above. Such an attitude, indeed, underlies the whole deductive approach of scientific method, with the scientist engaged on a path of specific discovery rather than of general exploration. In this sense, therefore, inner city neighbourhoods, or concentricity of town structure, or a hexagonal distribution of settlement, for example. are not so much 'there to be seen' but, rather, require a definite perspective on the part of the researcher.

The mix of cultural characteristics may be summarised in a particular life-style which will find spatial expression in an associated movement field or action space. The latter would seem a key explanatory variable in the extent and content of the image, and has been explicitly studied in Los Angeles (Orleans, 1973) and Cuidad Guayana (Appleyard, 1969), for example. The validity of any inter-group differences, however, rests on culture-fair techniques having been applied to elicit the image (see chapter 4).

The last component at the perceiving stage, current state, relates to particularity of circumstance, to the needs or moods of the moment, emotional involvement or physical or biogenic needs. Places, as well as people, are quite clearly perceived differently through 'rose-coloured spectacles' compared with a 'jaundiced eye' or even a 'Monday morning feeling', for instance. Haste, anger, hunger, illness – all highly colour the response to a particular environment, particularly if it is an individual's first, last or only contact. The passing tourist sees with different eyes from those of the resident native, for example, while a pursued prisoner attempting an escape dash acquires an even narrower image of the environment he is traversing (see McVicar, 1974, pp. 119–22). This highlights a broad inverse relationship between depth or image and degree of goal orientation.

In summary, then, perception as a process is far from being solely a mechanical response. It is very much a cultural and subjective process, 'a continuous tuning in, amplification, suppression and interpretation' of the observed world (Dennis, 1951, p. 150).

THE IMAGE

If perception as a process is an intervening filtering between man and the environment, as a product the term refers to the resultant intervening construct – the image – which is related to, although not a copy of, the objective environment. Three interrelated types of response from the processing centre are shown in the conceptual model.

The first response, the designative aspect, is informational in nature, concerned with description and classification – the basic 'whatness' and 'whereness' of the image. It is here that the mental map, concerned with basic properties such as distance, orientation, location or spatial variations, is best seen as a purveyor of the image. The appraisive aspect is one of appraisal or assessment. It incorporates both evaluation and preference, the former including some general or external standards, the latter reflecting a more personal type of appraisal, and affection, which is the emotional response concerned with feeling, value and meaning attached to the perceived. Degree of acquaintance and involvement in an environment will determine whether the engagement is at a perceptual or conceptual level. Contrast, for example, the design orientation of the tourist with the social involvement of the resident.

The third response component relates to predictions and inference of both a designative and appraisive nature giving to the image a depth, continuity, pattern or meaning beyond that justified by experience of a particular scene alone. The basis for this component is the sum of experiences of similar situations, in the same or other towns, inferential structuring from the inherent laws of organisation, and, thirdly, perhaps logic and faith. Lowenthal (1961, p. 251), for instance, quotes the example from Descartes where, looking down from a window, we see men and women, when in fact we perceive only parts of their hats and coats.

The image as described is the result of cognitive adaption to the potential condition of stimulus overload. That part of the city which is 'known' is made comprehensible through a process of reduction and simplification. When attention is turned to the content of the derived mental model or image, the most obvious component is the physical structure.

In his seminal work on *The Image of the City,* Lynch hypothesised that an individual simplified physical form by organising it in terms of five elements – paths, edges, districts, nodes and landmarks (Lynch, 1960, pp. 46 – 90). Paths are channels along which the observer moves; edges are non-path linear elements providing barriers to vision and outlines to areas; districts are distinctive areas of the city; nodes are strategic foci; landmarks are single, prominent elements. Although Lynch recognised that the image was a compound of physical attributes and meaning, he deliberately chose to concentrate on the role of form, developing the hypothesis that an individual's knowledge of the city is a function of its imageability. This concept he defined as

> that quality in a physical object which gives it a high probability of evoking a strong image in any given observer. It is that shape, colour, or arrangement which facilitates the making of vividly identified, powerfully structured, highly useful mental images of the environment.
>
> (Lynch, 1960, p. 9)

The empirical results accompanying his work, showing how the images of the central areas of Boston, Jersey City and Los Angeles were structured, vindicated his research design, which has subsequently been replicated in a variety of cultural settings.

Legibility or clarity plays an important role in the simplification and organisation of the physical form. Defined as 'the ease with which its parts can be recognised and can be organised into a coherent pattern' (Lynch, 1960, pp. 2–3), it is an important quality, particularly on initial contact with a scene. It is not to be confused with imageability, which quality implies an indelible imprint in the formation of which legibility is but one aspect. Clarity alone may denote the simple or obvious and, hence, ultimately, prove monotonous and boring. For continuing interest in physical form, a certain *lack* of clarity may be required. A degree of complexity or ambiguity is thus an important component of imageability (Rapoport and Kantor, 1967).

Knowledge, and mental recording, of structures may be related not only to distinctiveness of form, both in absolute terms and in a relative or locational sense, but also to qualities of visibility. Thus the exposure of a structure – its position relative to points of decision such as cross-roads and relative to the general line or cone of vision – is an explanatory variable. The importance of paths and serial vision in forming and knitting together the image is thus appreciated, whether this be the view from the road (Appleyard *et al.*, 1964; Carr and Schissler, 1969) or from street pavements (Lynch and Rivkin, 1959).

Although physical attributes are an obvious reason why structures are known, neither prominence nor architectural detail guarantee imageability and a place in the perceiver's mental model. 'It is the attribute of significance which gives meaning to neutral environmental happening' (Ittelson, 1960, p. 34). That is to say, for space to become place, senses other than the visual and meanings other than the concrete may have to be invoked. Thus, it is questionable whether the visual or design qualities of buildings or townscape can be enjoyed for their own sake, for, except at the preliminary and temporary stage of sensation, visual experience is accompanied by some level of meaning experience. Although it has been suggested that in perception identification of an object precedes the attribution of meaning (Vernon, 1962), logically it is difficult to separate the processes since identification is only possible in terms having experiential relevance to the individual. Physical or visual form is thus identified or given meaning through some combination of usage (functions fulfilled), emotive (value or taste involved) and symbolic (ideas, sentiments represented) significance.

Attributes of physical form are more meaningful when they reinforce usage or activity patterns. In short, a church should look like a church and be used as such. Congruence between form and activity is particularly important in the early learning stage and in terms of general orientation and comfort. When form does not visually express an activity pattern, then it is the latter which will dominate a person's meaningful knowledge, perhaps even eliminating the attributes of form (Steinitz, 1968). Thus, both complexity and ambiguity may be reduced, and coherent structuring made possible, by identifying with the behavioural significance of the form. Symbolism is important for similar reasons.

Symbols play a vital parsimonious role in making the city comprehensible in that, by increasing the number of connections between 'bits' of information, they correspondingly increase both redundancy and predictability. The complexity of sensory information is reduced accordingly (Rapoport, 1969). Whole cities may thus be 'captured' by a summary in terms of particular attributes, analogies or personifications.

Whether seen as a whole or in its constituent parts, the city is a symbol of our culture and group cultures, reflecting its values, expectations, hopes and fears. This has been so since the beginning of urban life. The dwelling unit of ancient cities, its temple, and over-all form were all designed with an archetypal symbolism, an expression of religious or cosmological order in contrast to the arbitrariness of nature. Even city walls acted initially as a religious bounding of space before they were used for defensive purposes. The modern city is no less an artefact of symbolism, reflecting in particular the emphasis placed by urban man on material and economic values. Witness the status element in the competitiveness to erect tall – preferably the tallest – buildings in downtown locations, in shop fascias, or in house and car ownership, and in material possession generally.

Man, then, is very much a symbolic animal. Moreover, from the point of view of image formation if, as has been shown, man symbolises the environment which he engages, it is logical to assume, given acquaintance or involvement, that those symbols themselves may become stimuli to which he then responds. Given such a conceptual rather than perceptual level of response, this is a further reason why the physical stimuli *per se* do not exert an influence on the image directly proportional to their objective prominence. Accordingly, the concept of imageability cannot be defined in specifically physical terms.

SUMMARY

From the above discussion, certain characteristics of the image may be summarised. Firstly, it is a partial and simplified representation. Moreover, it is also distorted, being schematic or constructed to psychic or social metrics which are not necessarily isomorphic to the objective environment. Thirdly, the image is idiosyncratic, the environmental stimuli having evoked different responses in each individual. This means that, at one level, there are as many images as there are individuals, with each living in 'a personally apprehended milieu' (Lowenthal, 1961, p. 249). On the other hand, the individual's perceptions and attitudes are influenced by the society and place to which he belongs. And, as has been shown, the sharing of similar needs, ideals and loyalties induces common or group images. This theme runs through Boulding's early work on *The Image,* where the term 'public image' was used and defined as the 'basic bond of any society, culture, sub-culture or organisation' (Boulding, 1956, p. 64). The same premise underlies the work of Lynch, who sought 'collective images'. More exactly, the overlap or correspondence between individuals' perceptions may be considered a measure of the proportion of 'common image' derived from group norms, compared with the proportion of 'unique image', which is idiosyncratic and unpredictable (Harvey, 1973, p. 34).

A further characteristic of the image, given the feedback to both perceiver and environment in what is a continuing, cyclical system, is its dynamic nature. A simple environmental model may be postulated. Exhibiting a logistic or S-shape curve, there is a relatively brief period of rapid accumulation of information during the early learning stage, which levels off as patterned behaviour becomes established. At the same time, the significance of physical form gradually yields to social characteristics. Beyond the upper flexure point of the logistic curve, retention of details of the mental image depends on the relative rates of information renewal and decay.

Such a simple learning model as just outlined, relating as it were to the middle of the seven ages of man, excludes consideration of both extremities of the life cycle. Logically the process begins with the young child learning the properties of space and environment as part of his maturation process (Piaget and Inhelder, 1967), and, after a life of many parts, ends with the passage of time and physical change having increasingly less relevance. To people in 'slipper'd pantaloon' the 'inward eye' continues to feed on 'after-images', seeing friends long gone and scenes now altered or disappeared. Whatever may have happened to the world outside, their reality stems from the intangible sense of the place – the sentiment and values invested in the world as it was when they were fully involved and not disinterested observers.

From the above discussion, it will be evident that the image has a utility, not only as an indispensable part of an individual's survival kit, but potentially as the crucial intervening variable when attempting to understand spatial behaviour and also in environmental design exercises. Thus, if the present urban environment does reflect largely untested assumptions about human preferences and behaviour by the professional planners, then perception and image studies involve an approach which may close the gap between the planner, the policy maker and the public. Observing use or noting evaluation and preferences through various projective techniques may offer meaningful 'participation' in an era when the role of urban planning has been increasingly questioned from within and attacked from without. Certainly, questions of orientation, mental structuring and optimal perceptual inter-action with the environment become increasingly important as urban man sees his habitat, itself a recent phenomenon, undergoing rapid change. The concepts of legibility and imageability would seem to hold considerable relevance. The planning and policy implications of image studies will be specifically examined in the latter part of this work.

The image may also be considered an integral part of the behavioural approach to the understanding, and thus predicting, of human spatial behaviour. This is self-evident from the observation that decisions are taken on the basis of what is *believed* to be the best – however defined – from among alternatives that are *known*. This is applicable whether the behaviour concerns work, recreation, shopping or choice of residence. Such behavioural links will be discussed where relevant although the emphasis of this work will be on the image *per se*. First, however, further attention will be given to a discussion of methodological problems.

4 Measuring Environmental Images

In many ways the most crucial issue in the study of environmental images was and is that of measurement. While the conceptual attraction of the image approach has not been denied, doubts as to its viability and feasibility as an operational approach have been expressed, threatening even to halt the growth of interest in such an approach. Therefore, initially, considerable attention was of necessity focused on solving the problems of measurement, perhaps to the detriment of other aspects of image studies.

The confusion that existed over problems of measurement was not helped by the fact that initiatives in the study of environmental images have sprung from a variety of disciplinary sources, each tending to have its own methodological and philosophical stance. Although this diversity has lent a certain richness and texture, it has also proved a source of problems, the various approaches having been based on a variety of theoretical perspectives, often implicit and not explicitly clarified. A corollary of this theoretical diversity is the wide variety of methodologies used to measure environmental images, methodologies that are often at variance or even contradictory in the assumptions on which they are based and the evidence which they produce.

Thus studies of environmental images have used a variety of methods invented and used by a variety of disciplines – sociology, psychology, anthropology, political science, geography. These methods include various types of survey and attitude questionnaires, laboratory and clinical techniques devised by psychologists, participant observation methods, and content and textual analyses of a variety of media presentation. These have both strengths and weaknesses: for example, it is argued that 'one-shot' attitude surveys can lead to distortion and contradiction through over-simplification (Proshansky, 1972; Tuan, 1973), yet it is often only by the use of such methods that representative samples of populations can be considered. Initially, in the 1960s, measurement methodologies were either invented within geography or derived from psychology and measurement theory, bringing strong associations with positivism. In the 1970s, with increasing interest in the role of the media in relation to image formation, more attention is being devoted to methodologies devised in the context of sociological studies of the media. In general, methods used have involved differing and at times conflicting assumptions of the processes and products of measurement.

In this chapter the main focus is on approaches that attempt the direct measurement of images by the use of specific methods, rather than recreating images from data recorded for other purposes. (For a consideration of the problems associated with the latter approach, see Giddens, 1976. These problems are touched upon in succeeding chapters.) Even given this limitation, it is difficult – some might argue impossible – to generalise from these various methods to common general principles that can be used to conceptualise the process of measuring environmental images. The task is made more difficult by conceiving the image as possessing designative, appraisive and prescriptive attributes. It involves attempting to generalise from methods as diverse as drawing maps of one's neighbourhood to assigning numbers to locations to evaluate the degree to which they possess a variety of attributes. But it is important to attempt this generalisation, to set up criteria against which can be guaged the specific methods and techniques used in measuring environmental images.

The essence of the problem is that, by definition, 'environmental images' exist as psychological entities 'inside our heads'. They lack a physical existence – in the usual meaning of that phrase – and thus cannot be measured in the way one would measure the attributes of a physical object. It is this aspect of images, their existence as psychological rather than physical entities, that lies at the core of the measurement problem which must be overcome if images are to be measured in a valid and reliable way.

One approach, reflecting a powerful, if recent, tradition in geography, is to consider measurement as a modelling process: that is, a process whereby one attempts to map observations about reality, in this case the psychological reality of the image, into a mathematical system of given properties. Following Harrison and Sarre (1971), the measurement process can be conceived as made up of three stages – specification, scaling, and generalisation and inference – each of which is affected in important ways by the 'unobservable' character of the image.

SPECIFICATION

Specification refers to conceptualising the image as a measurable form, made necessary because the image lacks a convenient physical form. This implies that, ideally, one does two things. First, one conceptually links the image to some underlying formative processes and/or behaviour to be explained. Second, one conceptually links the image to some 'observable' indicators that are measurable by using a selected measurement method. This may involve conceptualising, say, the designative aspects of the image literally as a 'mental map', or the appraisive aspects of the image as a multi-dimensional cognitive model on whose dimensions various places are evaluated. These conceptual linkages are necessary if measurement is to yield relevant information. But to conceptualise the image does not entail any necessary metaphysical belief in its existence; rather one proceeds as *if* it exists because it is useful to do so.

For geographers interested in studying and measuring environmental images, two courses of action are open to attempt to overcome this problem of specification. One involves devising theories of mental structure and testing their validity by measurement. This was the strategy initially adopted by geographers in the early stages of image study and one that is still much used. While it can lead to problems, mainly resulting from neglect of the relevant psychological and measurement theory, this neglect was much more in evidence in the initial stages of image studies than it is now. A powerful attraction to geographers studying environmental images is that such methods are strong in terms of spatial concepts.

The alternative is to adopt existing theories and methods, primarily from psychology, which, while not without problems, has proved the only practical course for most geographers and applied researchers. It was adherence to this approach that led to the adoption of the variety of approaches outlined above. To choose from available measurement methodologies requires judgement, particularly given the variety of potential methods, for choosing from approaches often designed for other tasks opens the risk to specification errors (although in the context of measuring images these can never be absolutely ruled out). The alternative of borrowing from existing methodologies has been increasingly taken up: various questionnaire approaches, methods from psychology such as the Semantic Differential, Repertory Grid and Thematic Apperception Test, participant observation methods, have all made their debut in the context of measuring environmental images.

SCALING

Scaling is a process of assigning numbers to objects to represent attributes of those objects. While a comparatively straightforward process in the case of physical objects, this is not so with 'unobservable' images. A key point is that the actual objects are not measured, but rather one or more attributes of those objects – which in this case are images – which may be specified by either researcher and/or respondent (at the specification stage).

Considering measurement as a modelling process implies an isomorphism, ideally a strict one-to-one correspondence, between the properties of the object being measured and the numerical scale or operations used to represent them. Thus there are close links between the specification and scaling stages. However, in the case of 'unobservable' images one cannot see what one is measuring, which raises two types of problems. The first concerns the degree to which one's chosen methodology really measures the theoretical construct, the 'image', as conceptualised at the specification stage; that is, the validity of the measure. This is a crucial problem and will be returned to below.

The second problem concerns the researcher's adoption of an appropriate level of measurement: that is, whether he should select a nominal, ordinal, interval or ratio measurement scale. There is a broad trade-off involved here between the increasing sophistication of measurement and the range of potential statistical and quantitative analytic techniques that are applicable to, for example, interval rather than nominal scale data, and the increasing difficulties of respondents in handling these techniques as the sophistication of numerical scales increases. In practice, techniques range from recording the presence or absence of places or objects, a nominal scale, to requesting people to assign numbers to objects.

It is when people assign numbers to objects that questions of scale validity assume importance, although even map drawing techniques, for example, raise their own scaling problems, as will be seen below. Most psychologists would accept that, given an appropriate methodology, people can generate valid and reliable rank order scales. What is less clear is whether, in the context of measuring environmental images, people can make the judgements necessary to generate interval scales (Torgerson, 1958). It is argued that judgements are essentially comparative, and that therefore at best rank orderings, that is ordinal scale measures, are valid and reliable (Ellis, 1966).

This would seem to impose a barrier in terms of the type of quantitative and statistical analytic techniques and models that can be applied to such data, since many of these require assumptions of interval scale data. However, under appropriate conditions rank order scales can be assumed to have properties of interval scales; that is, one can proceed as if the scales truly were interval scales. For example, by using category scaling methods, whereby objects are assigned to categories of assumed equal size on each relevant dimension, scales are produced that can be handled as interval scales. More generally, recent attention has focused on the links between metric and non-metric scales, particularly in the context of multidimensional scaling approaches. Basically, as more and more constraints are placed on a non-metric scale (for example, a ranking), the nearer it approximates a true metric scale (for example, an interval scale).

Thus far it has been argued that environmental images can be measured but that, at best, this measurement process is an indirect one which relies for its validity on an adequate theoretical specification of the links between technique, image, learning process and/or behaviour. However, a central problem that relates to both specification and scaling stages is to what degree does the result, the image as measured, reflect the particular choice of measurement method – to what degree is one measuring the image as specified? Clearly one way to approach the former aspect is by comparative studies using differing methodologies. The latter aspect is even less amenable to solution as to some degree it reflects the interaction between any given respondent and the chosen measurement method.

Basically there are two types of measurement procedure: unobtrusive and obtrusive. Unobtrusive measures do not involve the conscious participation of the individual being studied; for example, one might observe a person's behaviour without his knowledge and from this attempt to make some (albeit hazardous) inferences as to various properties of his environmental images. Obtrusive measures, on the other hand, do involve the conscious participation of the person being studied. Thus the respondent becomes an integral part of the measurement process. This point is made by Craik (1970, pp. 65–88) who recognises four issues to be dealt with in measuring environmental images or, as he puts it, in the comprehension of 'environmental displays': how to present the environmental display to observers (media of presentation); which behavioural reactions of observers to elicit and record (response formats); which are the relevant attributes of displays (environmental dimensions); whose comprehension to study (observers). Therefore a person's actual ability to comprehend a given method becomes crucial. Ample evidence already exists to show that there are systematic biases between people, for example in terms of socio-economic group or level of education, in their ability to handle various types of measurement methods used in investigating environmental images (see Rieser, 1972).

A useful way to look at the issues of person – method interaction is to view image measurement as a sign process (see Harvey, 1969*b*, who discusses this in terms of the theory of semiotics developed by Morris, 1964). This entails that image measurement is viewed as a reaction to a particular set of stimuli: that is, environmental circumstances as presented to a respondent. The mode of presentation can vary greatly in form and degree of structuring. Basically there are two types of sign process as regards stimuli – signal and symbol. A signal is a direct stimulus from the environment; the respondent is actually 'in the field'. There are formidable problems associated with this approach, both technical and financial. A symbol is a substitute for a direct signal: for example, it may be a map, photograph or verbal label relating to an area or place. The symbol is used to evoke a response and so measure the environmental image. In the measurement of environmental images, symbols are generally used as the stimuli. Many forms of stimuli and representational displays are available (Craik, 1970). However, these may be categorised into one of three types: iconic, in which the actual form and relationships of objects are maintained but at a reduced spatial scale; graphic; and verbal. Within these categories, different modes of stimulus presentation vary in the degree to which they are structured (see table 4.1). Different types of

TABLE 4.1

A TYPOLOGY OF METHODS OF STIMULUS PRESENTATION

Type of stimulus presentation	*Form in which presented to respondent* Structured* or Constrained	Less Structured* or Open
'Reality' (A)	Take respondent through actual route or area. Record required reactions at go and at return. Or measure sensory reaction, i.e. eye movement camera.	Unguided and undirected trip or exposure in actual area. Controlled for groups, i.e. experience/knowledge of area.
Iconic (B) continuous†	Series of photographs: describe what is in between recognised ones, or fit in order. Motion film of area; stop projection, ask what comes next.	Show a large selection of photos of area; respondent picks out those recognised.
Iconic (C) discontinuous†	Recognition of a series of photos taken at regular intervals; may also state if in/out of area.	As above. Spatial continuity will emerge, especially with probing.
Graphic (D) continuous†	Present with street map, draw a line around specified area, i.e. central city or home area.	Sketch area on blank sheet of paper. Little control of respondent's interpretation of requirements.
Graphic (E) discontinuous†	Identify individual streets and elements directed on map.	As above. Extent of continuity will emerge from the sketch.
Verbal (F)	Object or place named or described. Respondent explains how to get there if recognised. Repeat until composite image.	Describe requested area, i.e. name or describe streets, places, etc. and their locations.
Verbal discontinuous†	Names or descriptions of places on individual cards. Pick out those of specified area recognised.	As above. Will depend on description and extent of probing.

* Structured/less structured refers to how specific the stimuli are and so how constrained are the responses.

† Continuous/discontinuous applies to the spatial form inherent in the different kinds of stimuli presentation. This will depend on secondary controls and the amount of inference made from responses.

Source: Rieser (1972), figure 2.

stimuli require different skills for recognition and manipulation. Clearly the way in which the respondent interprets the stimulus is crucial. This depends on two things: knowledge of the object or place that the symbol represents and recognition of, and an ability to handle, the symbolic language. If the symbolic language remains unrecognised, it may well be that the symbol is evaluated independently of the object that it represents.

As a result of these possible problems, one can think of a number of types of potential bias in responses where symbols are used to evoke images. The respondent may be unable to 'read' the symbolic language – for example, a person may be unable to 'read' a map. Secondly, the response may be to the symbol *per se* and not to the place that it supposedly represents – for example, one might react to a map as a work of art rather than as a symbol for places. Thirdly, and perhaps most crucially, the respondent may be unable to understand and manipulate the symbolic language in which the response is to be given – for example, asked to draw a map of his home area, he may not understand the basic principles of cartography. Moreover, there are wide interpersonal variations and variations between social groups in levels of literacy and command of language (Bernstein, 1971). This type of problem is also likely to occur if the response language is numerical, in which case the previously mentioned problems of scaling and the level of measurement that can be assumed valid must be considered.

GENERALISATION AND INFERENCE

Problems here are closely related to those of the two preceding stages of specification and scaling. Confidence in inferences depends on confidence in the quality of data collected. The main problems at this stage relate to sampling; that is, whether rules have been specified for the selection of respondents such that the chosen sample gives an unbiased and representative sample of the wider population.

One myth, which is best early dismissed, is that while many image studies refer to individuals' images of environments, this does not mean that one is restricted to making unique statements about one person. Rather, one seeks to generalise from groups of individuals in terms of the structure, content and role of their environmental images. The extent and nature of generalisations that can be made are problems of sampling, in which two main approaches can be considered: conventional sampling theory and an alternative approach, primarily developed in clinical psychology.

Conventional sampling theory seeks to draw a (random) sample from a population and make inferences from certain characteristics of the sample to the population at a specified level of statistical confidence. The basis of inference depends on drawing on a sample of sufficient size to abolish systematic variations in respondents' characteristics that might bias measurement and results. This is the crux of the matter because in studies of environmental images, with the heavy demands on time these make of both researcher and respondent, it is often unrealistic to expect to generate a large random sample of respondents. Frequently, one is forced to work with small, self-selected samples of respondents; such samples are, by definition, non-random. At the same time, it is manifestly unrealistic to expect to specify the characteristics of any one person in sufficient detail to account for variation in all aspects between all people. It is a common situation in environmental image studies to have to work with small, non-random samples of people, the worst of both worlds. While screening procedures, a form of purposive sampling, are used to filter out specific interest groups, be they town planners, old age pensioners or White Anglo-Saxon Protestants, they do not remove the fundamental problem of the relation of sample to population and consequent validity of the 'consensus' image produced (for example, see Pocock, 1976*a*). Basically this problem reduces to a situation of small sample size, a non-random sample and large intra-sample variation; at this point conventional sampling theory ceases to be useful.

An alternative approach is a sampling strategy developed mainly in the context of clinical psychology, although this has its own problems. Clinical psychologists are concerned with the impacts of treatment on patients and so have developed a sampling strategy that is heavily reliant on a time – series approach. Having a captive audience, problems of repeated measurements with the same person do not arise. Unfortunately this is not usually the case in studies of environmental images and such longitudinal data are rarely available.

Accepting this problem, the rationale of this alternative sampling approach is that there are as many hypotheses to test about an individual as there are perceived associations among the attributes of that person. From this stage, one can go on to compare individuals to see if similarities exist, for example, in terms of the content or structure of their environmental images, and relate these similarities in psychological characteristics to more easily measured personal attributes, such as various socio-economic characteristics. In this way, hypotheses can be tested at the group level and inferences extended to the group level. But what one cannot validly do is to go on and make inferences about individuals or groups in some wider unspecified population; the validity of inferences stops at the level of the inductively derived groupings.

At this point, having discussed problems of inference and generalisation, it is appropriate to consider two issues that were briefly mentioned earlier: the validity and reliability of image measurement procedures.

RELIABILITY AND VALIDITY

Reliability is the degree to which it is possible to replicate measurements of images at various points in time and obtain the same answer: that is, a test – retest situation. When measuring physical objects, which at least in the short term are reasonably permanent and unchanging, this is a fairly minor problem and relates mainly to instrument or operator variation on successive measurements.

Image measurement at different points in time raises more serious and fundamental problems. A crucial, implicit assumption in a test – retest situation in measuring images is that these are stable and invariant with time. This may be so in certain cases, but in many cases this is a much less plausible assumption. People both forget and learn while environments change, and in some cases, such as urban environments, the rate of change may be rapid (see Toffler, 1970). Therefore in many cases it would be manifestly unrealistic to expect stable images.

Recognition of this point raises immense conceptual and practical problems. If one measures a person's environmental image at two points in time and obtains differing results, to what degree can the differences be attributed to cognitive change, or do they represent 'noise' variation arising from the nature of the measurement methodology? Ideally to resolve this question would require *a priori* that one could predict the direction and amount of cognitive change.

This highlights the need for a sound theoretical framework, an adequate specification of the links between the structure and content of the image and the generative processes that give rise to the image. To be able to predict the degree and direction of cognitive change would necessitate studies of individuals to a depth that seems impossible in the study of environmental images. Whether one would wish to be able to do so raises ethical issues, but practically, in the short-term future, that nettle need not be grasped as the level of sophistication required to predict precise cognitive change in environmental images lies far beyond our grasp.

In practice, methods of test – retest association or difference are used to assess the reliability of image measurements. But suppose there is an 80 per cent agreement between test and retest, how does one interpret the 20 per cent difference? Is it to be attributed to random measurement error or meaningful change in the image? This is a crucial issue and one which at present cannot be resolved.

Validity refers to the degree to which measurement methods actually measure the image as theoretically specified. That is, it relates the measurement of the actual theoretical concept, the image, to the degree to which the image measured merely reflects respondents' ability to understand and use the measurement methodology.

Again, the psychological, as opposed to physical, nature of the image causes problems in assessing the validity of image measurement methods, since the nature of the image means that attempts to validate measurements must be done indirectly and not directly.

One approach to this, as hinted above, is to use a variety of measurement methods and compare the overlap and differences in the resulting images. Perhaps a better way, assuming that the image underpins behaviour, would be to relate the image to behaviour, which in turn implies a specification of the theoretical links between image, behaviour and measurement procedures. Again this raises ethical issues, whether one ought to predict individual behaviour, and serious theoretical and practical problems of attempting to fuse image and behaviour in this manner. The usual way of resolving this issue is to assume rather than explore the relationships of image to behaviour.

Perhaps the most important point to establish is that despite the numerous problems encountered, environmental images can be measured, if not always as precisely as might be wished. Various measurement procedures are available. But methods designed to measure particular aspects of the image inevitably neglect other aspects. Single methods catch only a fraction of the image – to grasp its totality necessarily requires a variety of methods.

SUMMARY

The model of mental structure of the image that is selected is crucial to the image measurement process. In making this choice, it is imperative to consult the relevant portions of mensural and psychological theory. Much of the earlier work on regional and urban environmental images in geography was handicapped by its *ad hoc*, atheoretical nature. To be able to specify, measure and then validate measures of environmental images ideally implies a broad theoretical framework, on the one hand linking the structure and content of the image to the processes that produce the image, and on the other hand linking the structure and content to some form of observable behaviour. That is, the image must be seen in both its social and functional context.

The chosen model of the image must lead logically to a method that enables the researcher to quantify or measure certain aspects of this mental structure: that is, one must have an identified model. Again, this absence of explicit links between measurement procedures and a model of mental structure seriously affected some early studies of environmental images.

However, despite such problems it remains true that one can measure environmental images, although the relationship between measurement methodologies and the image as measured is a subtle one. It is important to remember that the results of image studies discussed in subsequent chapters should be viewed in this light.

5 Designative Aspects of the Image

The basic structure or designative nature of the image is a subset of reality as mediated by the individual. Given the complexity of the environment and the limitations of elicitative techniques discussed in the previous chapter, it is evident that caution must accompany the description of any mediation. The relative importance of the structural, natural or social features of the environment depends, in the first instance, on the type of question posed (Rozelle and Baxter, 1972). It also depends on whether the recall is of an area, be it of a whole city or a distinctive part of a city, or of a perceived journey. The question of scale is ever present, for the individual lives and moves and has his being in a hierarchy of social spaces (see Buttimer, 1969) or existential space (Norberg-Schulz, 1971, pp. 27–36). Accordingly it is logical to assume that the individual has an interlocking hierarchy of mental schemata or images (Lee, 1964, p. 23). Attention here will be primarily at the city level, first on the image elements themselves and then on characteristics of their spatial disposition.

IMAGE ELEMENTS

Although environmental experience is a totality contributed to by all sense modalities, the dominance of the eye means that the contents of the image are largely visual. To the person possessed of all faculties, the roles of sound, smell and feeling are supportive, adding contrast, continuity and meaning to the visual scene. The contribution and nature of this supportive role is only properly appreciated in controlled experiments when the effect of deprivation of particular senses can be measured. In one such experiment in Boston, for instance, removal of the sonic environment produced a cityscape 'surrealistic in its peacefulness', but one which at the same time was sad, lacking contrast and almost two-dimensional (Southworth, 1969, p. 61).

From a visual or design point of view Lynch (1960) showed that the image of the city was organised and remembered by the selection of particular landscape elements – landmarks, districts, paths, nodes and edges. Together they provide for the legibility and imageability of the city, qualities which are desirable on both pragmatic and aesthetic grounds. The findings of Lynch's classic work in Boston are reproduced in figure 5.1, where the results of mapping and verbal techniques may be compared and interpreted in the light of the discussion in chapter 4.

In going beyond the standard treatment of buildings, streets and quarters of conventional architecture – planning texts, Lynch was concerned with an existential dimension, the environmental image being composed of a few basic elements arising from man's activities. An existential type of approach was later followed by Norberg-Schulz (1971, pp. 17–27), whose three basic elements of place, path and domain were given a Gestalt interpretation. Places, linked with the concept of proximity, were defined as goals or foci where the meaningful events of existence are experienced; paths, linked with continuity, provided the organising axes; domains, as areas of particular character, were linked with the concepts of enclosure and similarity and considered as relatively unstructured ground on which places and paths appeared as more pronounced figures. The whole was conceived as architectural space, that is to say, a concretisation of existential space.

Norberg-Schulz's work offers an explanation for the difficulty which some studies have encountered in describing public images in terms of Lynch's five landscape elements (table 5.1). Although the Lynchean elements and techniques have been widely applied, some discrepancies have occurred which are attributable neither to inherent city character nor to differences in research design.

The element edge is weakly present in a majority of cases. Although an obvious design element with a distinctive bounding or enclosing property, the dividing line is apparently unimportant compared with the contrast in character or quality of the parts it separates. Secondly, the element node is variously present according to whether the study has a design or social – functional emphasis. A building, for instance, may be both a landmark by appearance and node by function; on the other hand, it may be distinctively neither, so that in a study of Bath,

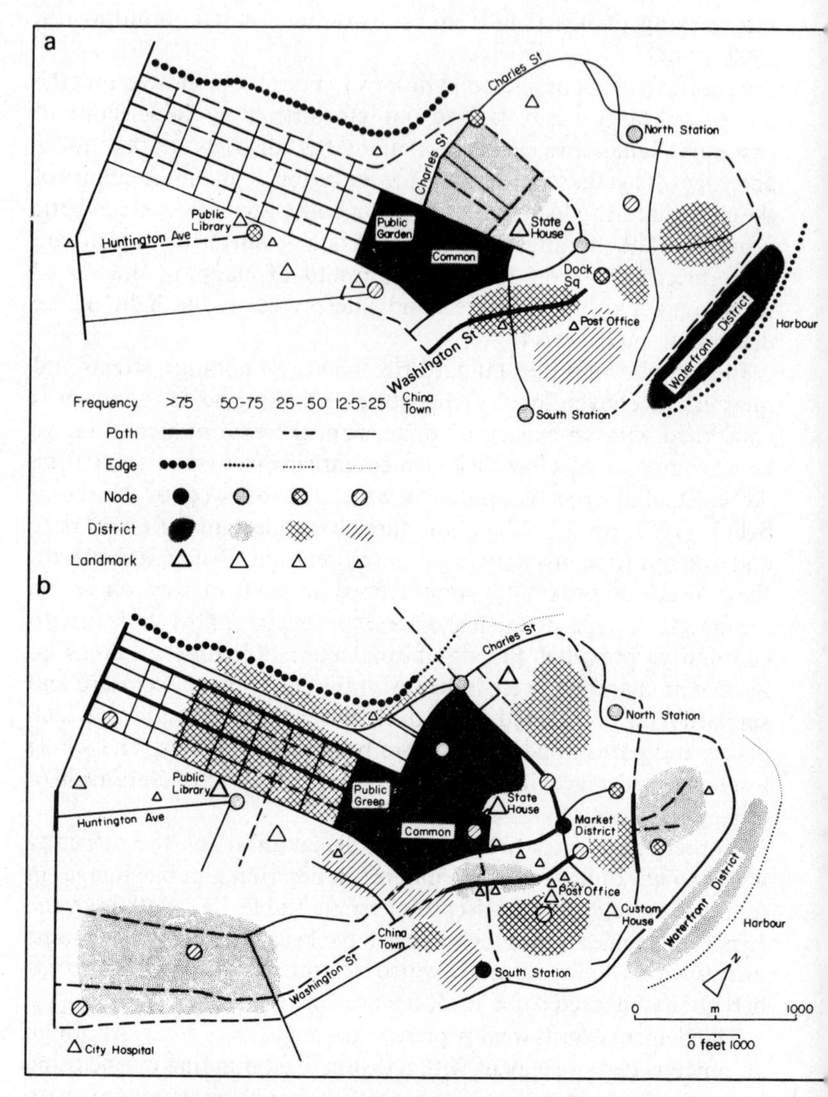

Figure 5.1 The collective image of Boston derived from: a, sketch maps; b, verbal interviews (Source: Lynch, 1960, pp. 146)

TABLE 5.1

IMPORTANCE OF LANDSCAPE ELEMENTS IN CITY IMAGE STUDIES IN EUROPE AND NORTH AMERICA

City	*Sample size*	*Paths*	*Landmarks*	*Districts*	*Nodes*	*Edges*
Boston[1]	30	+	*	*	+	+
Jersey City[1]	15	+				
Los Angeles[1]	15	*	+		+	
Chicago[2]	42	*	*	*		
Englewood[3]	44	*	*	*	+	
Amsterdam[4]	25	*			*	
Rotterdam[4]	22	*	+		+	
The Hague[4]	25	*	+	+		
Rome[5]	47	*	*	+	*	
Milan[5]	41	*	*	*	*	
Birmingham[6]	167	*	*		*	
Hull[7]	95	*	*		*	
Goole[8]	20	*	*	*	+	
Ellesmere Port[8]	25	+	+	*		
Stourport[8]	20	*	+	*	+	
Market Drayton[9]	43	*	*			
Durham[10]	94	*	*	+		

* = very important
+ = important

All relate to mapping exercises.

Source: 1 Lynch (1960); 2 Saarinen (1969); 3 Harrison and Howard (1972); 4 de Jonge (1962); 5 Francescato and Mebane (1973); 6 Goodey *et al.* (1971); 7 Goodey and Lee (1971); 8 Porteous (1971); 9 Goodchild (1974); 10 Pocock (1975).

for instance, an additional element simply named 'function' was used to interpret more realistically the collected data set. Some studies have combined the element node with that of landmark – Norberg-Schulz's 'place' implicitly combines both – while another has classified node along with district as a type of area feature, which suggests that scale is an additional complicating factor.

Evidence suggests that the element edge, valuable only for its bounding property and without activity or functional significance, has been elicited, emphasised – perhaps almost created – by design-oriented studies, especially where the end product is in map form. Paths and nodes are fundamentally usage or activity oriented, concerned with 'moving man', and only incidentally design-oriented. The former element is crucially important in providing the platform from which to knit together in coherent sequence what would otherwise be spatially discontinuous knowledge. The city image is therefore acquired and sustained by an underlying network representing the individual's movement field or activity space. Among the elements, therefore, paths might be considered 'supports' rather than stimuli or cues (Golledge and Zannaras, 1973, p. 88). The intermediate position of the element node can now be appreciated. It is the focus of paths; as such it benefits from exposure or visibility, but this does not guarantee that the revealed design qualities will be deemed significant by the individual: they may be used rather than appreciated.

Landmarks and districts are unequivocally design elements, although differing in nature and scale. This is not to imply, however, any social significance for such elements or one-to-one relationship between physical prominence or distinctiveness with memorability and imageability. In a study of central Birmingham, for instance, the two outstandingly tall blocks, one rising to almost 500 feet, figured weakly in the public image (Goodey *et al.,*1971, p. 44). Findings generally show that architectural distinctiveness is not very memorable in itself (for example Sieverts, 1967, p. 283); in the words of Smith (1974*b*, p. 955) 'architectural evaluation is a minority sport', the pursuit of professionals and tourists. For the majority, forms needs to be allied with some functional use or symbolic meaning for effective imageability.

SPATIAL CHARACTERISTICS

Given the existential basis to the Lynchean typology, it has been emphasised that the characteristics of townscape elements are derived partly from their disposition. Knowledge of the urban structure therefore consists not only of the elements or attributes *per se*, but also of spatial characteristics in terms of distance, in relative location and in directional relationships.

Distance, the key geographical variable, is traditionally measured in physical terms of miles or kilometres, or functionally in terms of effective cost, time or effort. Recent research has revealed that some generalisation is apparent when the variable is cognitively transformed. A series of projective exercises have shown cognitive distance to be related to town form and structure in general, and to be a function of attributes of the route and destination or end points in particular (Briggs, 1973; Stea, 1969*a*). Interpretation, however, should always be qualified by the type of elicitation, whether a 'virtual trip' of a perceived journey or a series of straight-line or crow-flight estimates. While the former may demand no more than memory recall of a particular experience, the latter is important in that it implies that the respondent is drawing on some cognitive representation of the whole city (Canter, 1975, p. 6).

Intra-urban cognitive distance is generally greater than the objective distance, regardless of city size (Canter and Tagg, 1975) or transport mode – walking (Lee, 1970) or driving (Golledge *et al.*, 1969), or whether time (Thompson, 1963) or straight-line estimates (Pocock, 1972*a*) are used. It also appears that mental over-estimation declines with increasing physical distance, such that while shorter distances seem further, longer distances may seem nearer, than they are in reality. A distance of between six and seven miles was the point of changeover in this relationship in London; a breakpoint of half that magnitude was suggested in distance estimates in the compact city of Dundee. Characteristics other than magnitude of distance, however, intrude to complicate the measure.

The general layout and topography of a city are important in the extent to which they present an inherent legibility or Prägnanz, permitting the respondent to cognise a simple structure and thus form the basis for subsequent introspection and action. A river or waterfront and a road or rail network are crucial elements in this respect, providing reference lines for conceptual structuring. Thus cities with a formal structure, typically older ones with a major river as a dividing topographical feature, for example London or Glasgow, show less over-estimation and greater consistency compared with cities lacking obvious formal structure, for example Edinburgh or Tokyo (table 5.2).

Linearity of the route influences distance estimates for perceived journeys in that the greater the number of corners or turns, the greater the length of the perceived journey. Road junctions, being points of decision, have a similar lengthening effect, as does absence of clearly perceived routes or presence of perceived barriers for the 'virtual trip'. The extent to which the route is divisible into distinctive cognitive segments is also important. Although it has been suggested

TABLE 5.2

SUMMARY PATTERN OF DISTANCE ESTIMATES IN SELECTED CITIES

City	*No. subjects*	*No. points*	*Mean actual distance*	*Mean estimated distance*	*Standard deviation*	*Linear regression** $(Y = AX + B)$
Glasgow	50	5	2.67	3.97	0.76	$0.45X + 2.72$
Heidelberg	24	7	2.50	3.15	1.02	$0.70X + 1.41$
London	25	5	3.96	4.77	1.74	$0.74X + 1.84$
Sydney	23	12	13.61	17.19	7.70	$1.12X + 1.19$
Nagoya	18	10	5.33	7.51	3.57	$1.27X + 0.77$
Edinburgh	35	7	1.28	1.92	0.88	$1.29X + 0.27$
Tokyo	64	11	6.89	10.59	5.00	$1.39X + 1.03$

* Regression = mean estimates against actual distance (X).

Cities are arranged in order of regression slope, with those giving a decrease in overestimation against length above those which show a general overestimation of distances.

Source: Canter and Tagg (1975).

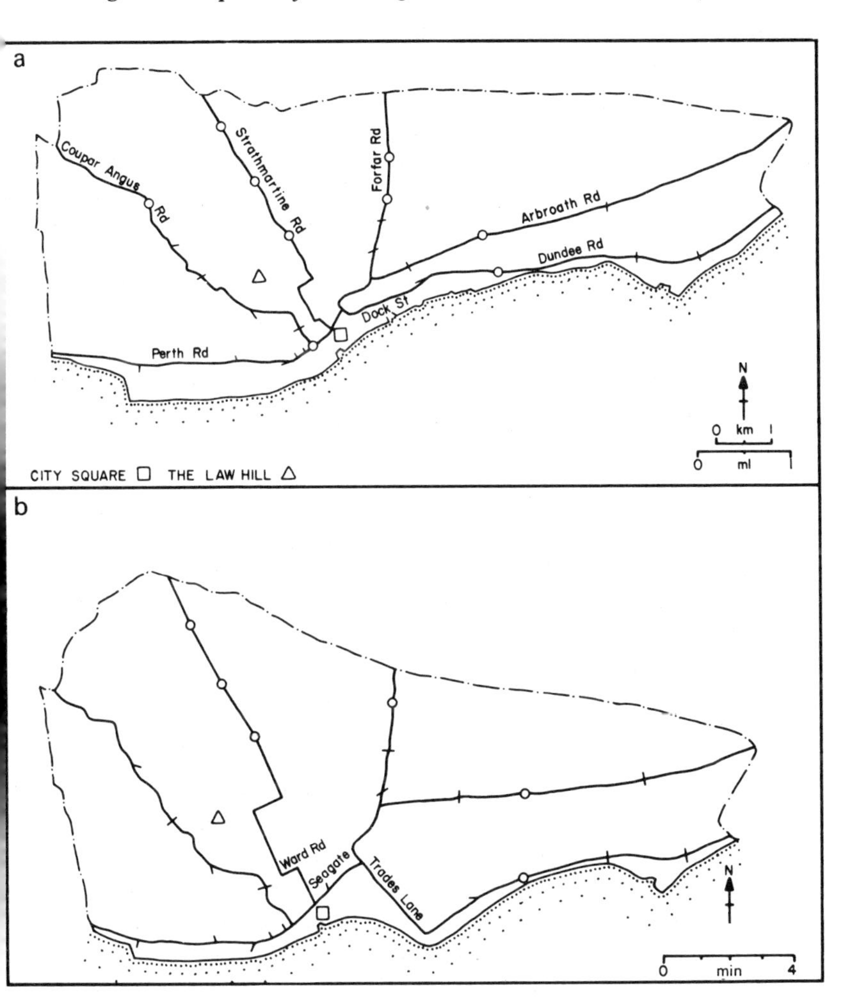

Figure 5.2 Time – distance in the city of Dundee: a, Roads and points at which timings taken b, Time – distance transformation, based on average of recordings on inward journeys arriving City Square between 8.45–9.00 a.m. during May, 1971 (Source: Pocock, 1972*b*, p. 121)

that divisibility is directly correlated with perceived distance (Stea, 1969*a*, p. 240), intra-urban findings point to an inverse relationship. Certainly the increasing stimulus complexity towards the inner part of cities – the greater density and variety of land use and building form – together with traffic impediments and reduced speeds, mean that distances are cognised as longer. Consistent with this are the findings within central London, where bus travellers exhibit an increase in overestimation of distance compared with underground travellers; the greater the use of the underground system, the greater is the tendency to congitive contraction (Canter, 1975, p. 24). Suburban townscapes, in contrast, with their greater uniformity and relatively unimpeded movement, evoke less arousal, and perceived distances are accordingly reduced. In its extreme form environmental monotony may induce actual gaps in environmental knowledge, as when commuters and long-distance drivers cannot recall having navigated particular sections of the highway (Tuan, 1975, p. 207). The typical contrast in mobility between centre and periphery in a radially organised city produces a time – distance map such as is illustrated in figure 5.2. It is interesting to note its close approximation to the mental map of the same city interpolated from distance estimates (see figure 5.3b).

Distance judgements are also influenced by the characteristics of the end points, the goals of travelling. A valency or reward hypothesis appertains, distances shrinking with perceived reward, however specified — whether degree of attractiveness, desirability, familiarity, emotional involvement, etc. Shops or retail centres have been obvious elements to test this hypothesis. An early study of different areas in San Francisco showed that positive attributes of a shop shortened perceived distance, whether physical distance or driving time (Thompson, 1963). In Wolverhampton (Brennan, 1948) and Cambridge (Lee, 1962) the significant preference for convenience goods shops on the town-centre side of the shopper's residence has been interpreted as a shortening of perceived distances in this direction induced by the general attraction of the city centre. This bias, supported by evidence from a third city, Dundee (Lee, 1970), prompted the hypothesis that mental distance may be a function of direction, dependent on the relative evaluation of the two points at either end of the journey. Evidence of a general foreshortening of inward journeys is equivocal, however. In Columbus, Ohio, a significant bias to foreshortening outwards was reported (Briggs, 1973), but before interpreting the contrast as resulting from different roles and accessibility of American downtown areas, reference may be made to the eccentric position of Lee's focus, and to the fact that the Columbus exercise was more akin to crowflight estimates.

It is logical to consider the valency hypothesis as a pluralistic one, with judgement functions varying not only on an interpersonal basis but also between different types of element. A general survey of neighbourhood facilities in Baltimore, Maryland, showed that desirable elements, such as school, library, post office or park, were perceived closer to the respondent's home than was the case in reality, while the reverse held for the less desirable elements, such as expressway interchange or parking lot (Lowery, 1973). The finding is consistent with the inherent tendency to inflate the size and increase the proximity of areas nearest and most important to the observer, a tendency operative equally at a local level as on a national or even international scale. Apart from, or as part of, the influence of relative location inducing such bias, the pervasive concept of social proximity or social distance means that sizes increase and distances shrink between areas of similar socio-economic character to the individual's home area; the reverse prevails for areas of inferior social, or functionally unrelated, characteristics. Thus, there may be an increase in the perceived distance between adjacent shopping and office zones of a city centre, but a reduction from an individual's neighbourhood to a similar or preferred one. Examples abound: the neighbourhood bias of a native interviewee in Ciudad Guayana (Appleyard, 1970*a*, p. 115); the middle-class elites of Westgate and Mountain Brow in Hamilton, Ontario, mentally shrinking their physical separation by the central business district and Niagara Escarpment (Watson, 1972); the population of Highgate, London, extending the 'village', with all its desirable qualities, towards their residence (Eyles, 1968); the inhabitants of Karlsruhe extending the town centre on the side nearest their residence (Klein, 1967) – all are indulging in the same cognitive process. 'Felt' distance is indeed crucial: in the words of Watson (1972, p. 5), 'nothing can overstress the importance of social distance in mental geography'.

Given the contrast in valence between end points, plus the influence of relative location where proximity and inflation are positively related, then it is little wonder that distances may be recorded and experienced as non-commutative, in effect A to B $\neq$ B to A. Who, for instance, has not experienced a homeward trip to be much shorter than the identical outward journey? The implication for the cognitive representation of the city as held by an individual is important. Not only is there a lack of uniformity of scale, with

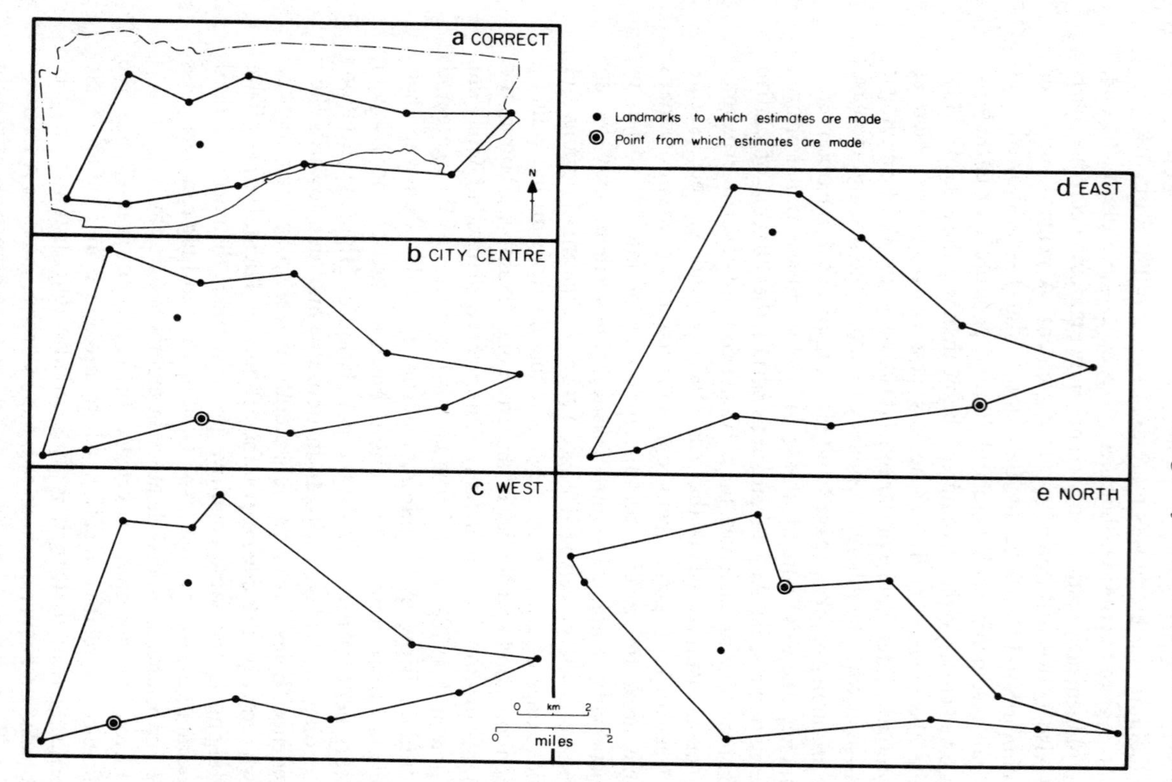

Figure 5.3 The changing perceived form of the city of Dundee. Mean conceptualisations of distance and orientation estimates to ten landmarks from different origins (Source: Pocock, 1972*a*)

cognitive structuring being non-Euclidean in nature, concerned with relational rather than positional points, but the structuring itself is an impermanent phenomenon. It is suggested that instead of, or perhaps in addition to, the structural Lynch-type mapped image, which is essentially a synoptic projection to which an individual applies total scanning, readjustment and 'polishing', an individual holds a more basic representation formed of the branching network in his action space (Pocock, 1972*a*). This simpler graticule, in constant use for purposeful action, undergoes topological deformation, perhaps hourly, as the individual moves about the city. The major deformations may be expected to be related to, and projections from, the key nodes – home, workplace, city centre – which are the decision-making points in an individual's action space. The influence of perceived origin is illustrated in figure 5.3 which shows the mean conceptualisations from four separate recalls of distance estimates to a common set of landmarks from a common population. Interestingly the representation from the city centre is the most accurate; attention has already been drawn to the similarity of this projection to a time – map of the same city (figure 5.2). The proportionately greater exaggeration of nearer and smaller distances can be seen in the 'movement' of the one central landmark in the different projections.

THE MENTAL MAP

Discussion will now turn from projective exercises concerned with specific spatial properties to actual map drawing in order to illuminate additional designative characteristics of the image. Although here concerned with results of map drawing exercises, the term 'mental map' is equally applicable to results derived by verbal means and subsequently processed to appear in map form. In either case, the term refers to the spatial or skeletal framework rather than to the more rounded phenomenon of the image, and is based on the underlying assumption that the environment as an entity only properly or fully makes sense when the separate parts are mentally structured in some sequential or relational context. At the same time it is worth repeating that the tapping of those parts of the respondent's data store relating to locational characteristics does not imply the inviolate existence of one composite map somewhere in the respondent's mind. In that the exercise is comprehensive and demanding, it is possible that respondents will be challenged to rationalise a situation which previously had lain in a dormant, even subliminal state. Indeed, it is probable that some material will be 'knitted' together for the first time. More correctly, therefore, it is the latent or potential map that is elicited by the lengthy introspection and overview required of such exercises. Recognition of this point may obviate misspent criticism of the validity of mental maps. Additionally, it is recognised that the free-recall technique, while easily applied and involving a minimum of intrusion by the researcher, nevertheless imposes a general filter on the individual's information store. In short, the response is constrained to physical attributes of the environment, and even then – annotation apart – to those items which are *mappable*. There are also other problems peculiar to the technique (Pocock, 1976*b*), but, with due recognition, the results of such exercises can further aid an understanding of how man mentally organises his environment.

The overall organisation of material may be summarised by map style. Categorisations based on the relative resemblance of the sketches to a map (Ladd, 1970) or even sorted according to developmental levels (Moore, 1973) are intuitively less satisfactory than a division combining two key dimensions – level of accuracy and type of element emphasised (Appleyard, 1970*a*). The latter dimension assumes that maps tend to consist predominantly of either sequential elements (notably roads) or spatial elements (individual buildings, landmarks or districts). In sequential maps the parts are more obviously connected, and the connections are dominant. In spatial element maps connections appear to be incidental between parts, which are characteristically scattered over the map. A subdivision of each type is recognised according to the level of accuracy and sophistication: that is, the extent to which the drawn map approximates to the topographical map of the city. Eight idealised 'map types' were thus derived in the study of Ciudad Guayana (figure 5.4). The types have subsequently been used elsewhere, for example in Small Heath, Birmingham (Spencer and Lloyd, 1974) and Market Drayton (Goodchild, 1974), and modified to incorporate a type to cater for a nuclear centre with radial route pattern (Pocock, 1975).

The literature reveals a general overall tendency to sequential style maps even allowing for obvious biases in particular town structure (Ciudad Guayana) or instructional set (Small Heath). Sequential

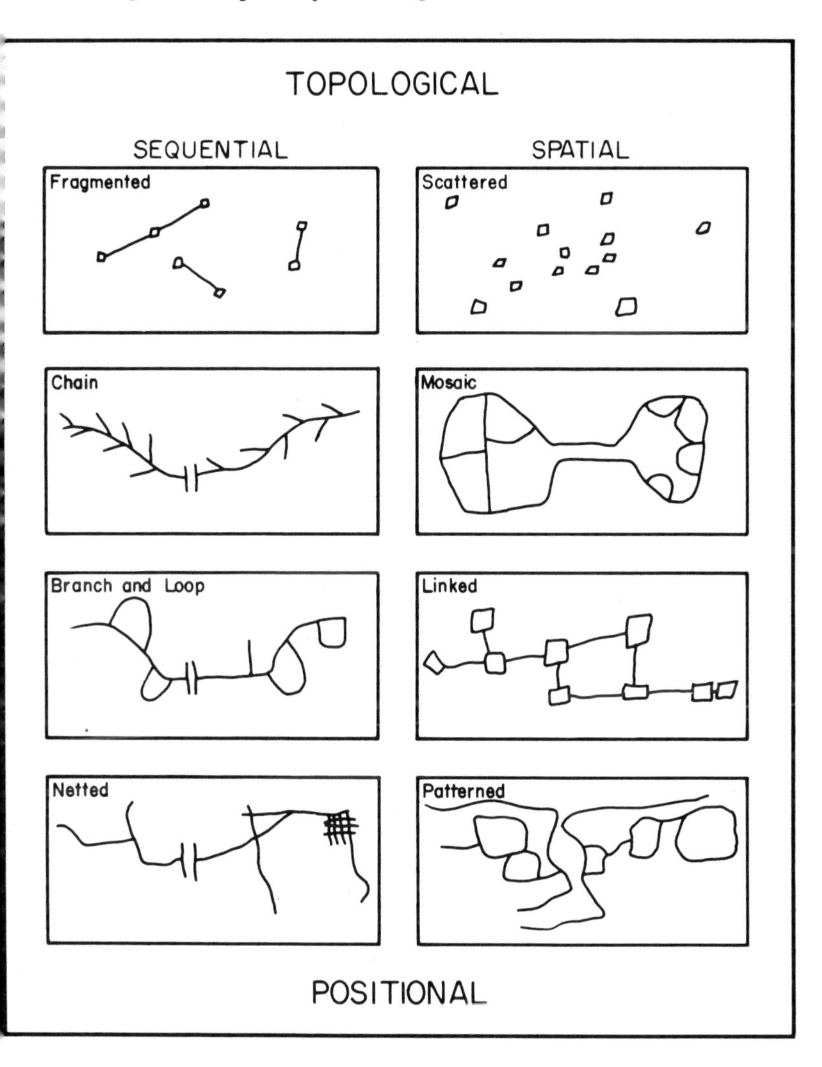

Figure 5 4 Typology of map styles, based on type of element and level of accuracy. Diagrammatic representation (Source: Appleyard, 1969, p. 437)

structuring together with a relative lack of sophistication characterise maps produced by working class and female respondents, which groups also show the highest initial rates of decline over the invitation to map. In addition to class and sex, map sophistication is positively correlated with education and temporal familiarity. The latter variable is a key one, given the experiential basis of environmental knowledge. Its importance is revealed, not only at an interpersonal level, but also by within-individual variation (Moore, 1974). That is to say, the same individual may produce maps of differing levels of representation or sophistication, the level directly relating to the degree of subjective familiarity with the particular areas depicted.

When the arrangment of the mapped elements is considered from the point of view of orientation, an experiential rather than objective projection is revealed. In an early paper on orientation, Peterson (1916) discovered that city dwellers orientated themselves by conspicuous urban features and not cardinal points. A recent exercise, in which adults were asked for a free-recall sketch map of their childhood 'home range', reported orientation to be 'highly varied and seldom compass (north) oriented' (Anderson and Tindall, 1972, section 1.1.4). As a result, the authors concluded that orientation tended in the direction of the city centre or of the primary path leading away from the home. Consistent findings are reported in Britain. In Goole, residents had to re-orientate themselves to appreciate a newly erected and cardinally orientated municipal indicator board (Porteous, 1971, p. 163). In Durham the choice of orientation in a map exercise was significantly related to place of residence or line of entry to the city centre for both inhabitants and visitors; conventional orientations, which totalled little more than one-third, increased with map sophistication. In Dundee, among the various orientations, accuracy was greatest among those from the home quarter or city centre (Pocock, 1972*a*).

An arrangement of elements from an experiential point of view is consistent with Orleans's (1973, pp. 126–7) concept of 'site recalcitrance'. If unique physical qualities do subvert the emergence of a common, over-all imagery, even among socially homogeneous groups, then it is equally logical to suggest that the environment habitually perceived along particular routeways will exhibit a similar recalcitrant quality. In turn, the mental organisation of the city may become subverted to a particular orientation.

Another well-attested everyday experience which is revealed in mapping exercises is the inherent tendency to 'better' the environment, to record a structure more uniform and less haphazard than that present in reality. Such good-figure tendency, prominent both among ancient maps and charts (Beazley, 1949, pp. 549–633) and in modern tourist or transport maps, is a key townscape ingredient (Johns, 1965; 1971). Moreover, such betterment, as part of the brain's simplifying logic, is not a feature confined to the learning phase, but is, rather, permanent and universal. Results show that good-figure tendency in fact increases with familiarity of the city concerned and with the degree of sophistication in the map drawn.

The inherent tendency to betterment contributes to the prescriptive element of the image, whereby an individual's mental representation has a depth, continuity, pattern or meaning beyond that justified by first-hand experience alone. Inference, a logical expectation or prediction based on generalisations learned from similar environmental experiences, is the second contributor to this prescriptive nature. Therefore, in that the perception process is 'a reduction in uncertainty' (Gibson, 1970), it is at the same time a growth in predictive ability. It has been acknowledged since Strabo's time that reasoning replaces observation to extend the image to terrae incognitae, although imagination and fantasy may blend with rationality, particularly when extrapolation straddles scale or cultural differences (Allen, 1976). Witness, for instance, the European engineer in Ciudad Guayana who, although having no difficulty in producing a coherent map of the settlement, inserted a railway between the steel mill and port – a logical, but wrong, deduction (Appleyard, 1970*a*, p. 112). More obvious examples are large-scale ones – such as the early inferred west – east alignment of the upper Nile in symmetrical sympathy with the known course of the river Danube in Europe; or, again, in the inferred shortened water distance between Iberia and Asia up to the time of Columbus, based on acceptance of the reference in the *Apocrypha* to the globe being sixth-sevenths land and only one-seventh water.

Inference and prediction are the outcome of the general learning process as a result of which each individual brings a set of experiences to any particular situation. The sum of urban knowledge and expectations constitutes a general learned model of the form of the city, which is then matched with any new experience of a new city (Appleyard, 1970*b*, p. 97). The rail traveller, for instance, may become aware of a definite sequence in the scenes heralding the approach of an industrial town (see Orwell, 1937, p. 18). For geographers in particular there is the question of the extent to which the entire urban area is mentally structured in a manner conforming

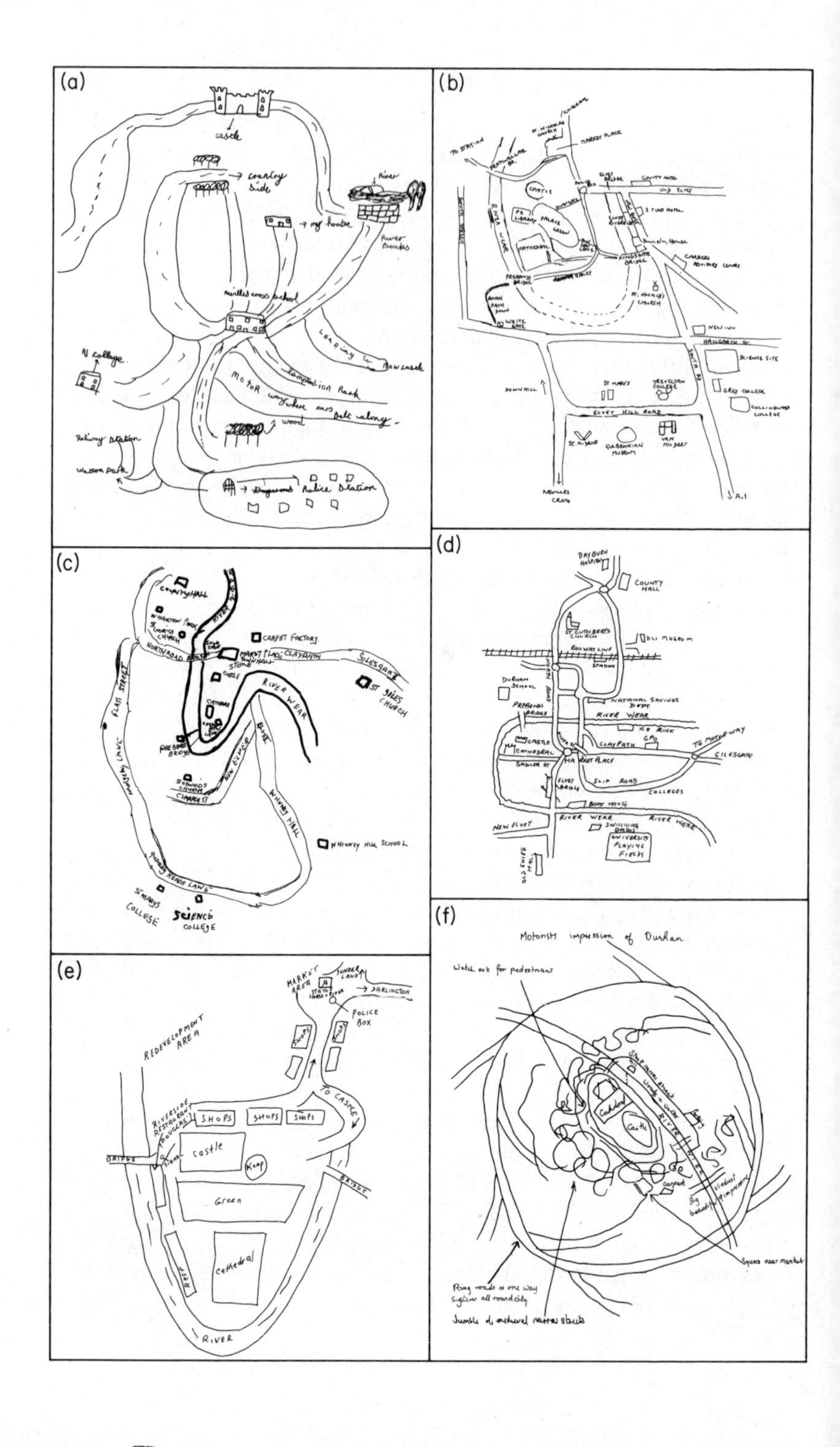

(a)
castle
country side
River
my house
River Banks
Leading to New castle
Motor way where cars belt along
N college.
Railway Station
Police Station
(b)
TO STATION
MARKET PLACE
CASTLE
LIBRARY
PALACE GREEN
CATHEDRAL
KINGSGATE BRIDGE
CAREERS ADVISORY CENTRE
PREBENDS BRIDGE
ST. OSWALD'S CHURCH
NEW INN
HALLGARTH ST.
SCIENCE SITE
ST MARY'S
TREVELYAN COLLEGE
GREY COLLEGE
COLLINGWOOD COLLEGE
ELVET HILL ROAD
ST. AIDANS
GULBENKIAN MUSEUM
VAN MILDERT
A.1
(c)
COUNTY HALL
WHARTON PARK
CARPET FACTORY
NORTH ROAD
MARKET PLACE
CLAYPATH
GILESGATE
ST GILES CHURCH
RIVER WEAR
CASTLE
CATHEDRAL
FLASS STREET
PREBENDS BRIDGE
NEW ELVET
CHURCH ST
WHINNEY HILL
WHINNEY HILL SCHOOL
ST MARYS COLLEGE
SCIENCE COLLEGE
(d)
COUNTY HALL
ST CUTHBERTS CHURCH
DLI MUSEUM
RAILWAY LINE
STATION
DURHAM SCHOOL
NATIONAL SAVINGS DEPT.
PREBENDS BRIDGE
RIVER WEAR
CASTLE
CATHEDRAL
CLAYPATH
GPO
TO MOTORWAY
GILESGATE
MARKET PLACE
SADLER ST
SLIP ROAD
COLLEGES
ELVET BRIDGE
BOAT HOUSE
NEW ELVET
RIVER WEAR
SWIMMING BATHS
UNIVERSITY PLAYING FIELDS
(e)
MARKET AREA
DARLINGTON
POLICE BOX
REDEVELOPMENT AREA
SHOPS
TO CASTLE
RIVERSIDE RESTAURANT
SHOPS
SHOPS
SHOPS
BRIDGE
castle
Keep
Green
BRIDGE
Cathedral
RIVER
(f)
Motorists impression of Durham
Watch out for pedestrians
Cathedral
Castle
RIVER
carpark
Square near market
Ring roads or one way system all round city
Jumble of medieval narrow streets

to one of the classic theories of physical structure (Golledge and Zannaras, 1973, pp. 87–92).

IMAGE VARIATION

The discussion hitherto has concerned the public or consensus image with only implicit reference to the fact that society is pluralistic, composed of different subgroups who respond differently to the same stimulus, and thereby construe images which differ both quantitatively and qualitatively. A host of personal and compound variables have been used to explain image variation. Of the latter, stage in life cycle, life style and social class have been taken as independent variables. Examples of the major types of image variation will be discussed below and include illustrations from a common mapping exercise applied to different subgroups of the population (figure 5.5).

Although age *per se* has not proved to be an explanatory variable, except where related to temporal familiarity or experience, the subgroups at either extremity of the life cycle clearly have distinctive involvement with the environment and emphasise different elements accordingly. The child's view of the city has received the more attention, having the experiential stages of child maturation as a theoretical starting point (see chapter 7). Here group images evolve as the uniqueness of each child's early experiences gives way to shared experiences in an expanding environment. The projection is egocentric, emphasising the home and local neighbourhood. Thus, for the nine-year-old boy the city revolves around his school (where the exercise was undertaken) and nearby house (figure 5.5a). The alternative structuring at this stage of development is to inflate the personally significant locale about the home and school, and to connect it loosely to the less well-known and schematically represented 'world' of the city centre.

◄ Figure 5.5 Mental maps of the city of Durham illustrating the different perceived worlds by different subgroups: a, Nine year old child; b, Final year undergraduate; c, Resident, working class; d, Resident, middle class; e–f,Tourists. Examples taken from mapping exercise with identical instructional set for each sample population (Source: Pocock, 1975, and unpublished research)

In children's maps elements are functionally rather than aesthetically determined, revealing a perception of the minute and detailed and of the incidental as compared with the adult world. In Harwich, for instance, the notable landmark of the lighthouse was much less important than the public toilets located at its foot (Bishop and Foulsham, 1973, p. 7). Again, in Harrisburg, Texas, prominent factories were omitted from sketch maps, while dog houses or house numbers were included (Maurer and Baxter, 1972, p. 371). Details of the 'floor' surface (Lukashok and Lynch, 1956), roadside features, and play or potential play areas reflect the child's particular engagement with the environment. With young children built structures are subordinate to elements of the social and natural environment (Spencer and Lloyd, 1974, pp. 45–7).

Spatial bias, which is present in everyone's mental organisation, is highlighted in the example of the student's map of the city on figure 5.5b. This 'personally apprehended milieu' is strongly sectorally organised, extending from college residence to university library. Even in this sector few non-university items are listed, and although the map just extends to the city centre the well-known landmark of the police box of the Market Place has been mislocated.

Long-term residents generally possess a more comprehensive and balanced image although there are degrees of competence in over-all organisation. Compare for instance the working-class effort (figure 5.5c), with its poorer geometric organisation, weak co-ordination and scale variation, with that of the middle-class example (figure 5.5d) whose competence is here expressed in a high degree of structural 'betterment'. Another characteristic of the middle-class is their interest in aesthetic and historic detail (Goodchild, 1974; Michaelson, 1970, pp. 115–9). Although social class is widely invoked to explain such contrasts, in that it is a composite variable – and, perhaps, of varying definition – more simply defined variables may pick up much of the same dimensional variation – occupation, travel mode, length of formal education, for instance.

Life style, as the expression of social class, may be expected to correlate with the spatial extent of the image, given the validity of the previously stated hypothesis of a usage – image link, where the number and variety of roles a person plays determines the number of parts of the city in focus. The polar positions along a place – non-place continuum are occupied in Webber's terms (1964*b*) by the localite and cosmopolite. The former, engaged in social worlds which are largely concentrated within a territorial neighbourhood around the place of residence, has a restricted image; the latter, with life spaces scattered throughout the city and beyond, has a much more comprehensive picture, even though it may contain enclaves of ignorance. Thus, in urban areas in England and Scotland the lower socio-economic groups have smaller 'home areas' (Community Attitudes Survey, 1969). In Los Angeles two poor and educationally deprived subgroups of negroes and Mexicans drew small and spatially confined maps of the city compared with sampled white subgroups (Orleans, 1973). There remains the question, however, to what extent the different response is a function of ability to respond to the elicitive technique. Certainly the two disadvantaged groups in Los Angeles had extensive journey-to-work patterns which were not reflected in their sketch maps.

Visitors possess another distinctive viewpoint and image compared with any resident subgroup. They see the environment, not through the filter of habituation in which meaning and social engagement have dulled alertness to physical appearance, but in a highly perceptive state. Visitors, particular if tourists, share a common current state with a high degree of expectancy focusing on design details and applying aesthetic judgements. They are, in short, 'sight-seeing'. Their grasp of, or interest in, over-all structure may be weak, however, and characteristically concentrated on a minute part of the city (figure 5.5e). Where a broader sketch of urban structure is attempted, the lack of temporal acquaintance may result in a map hardly distinguishable from that of a child's effort at the pre-operational stage (figure 5.5f).

The same environment is therefore experienced differently by different subgroups of the population. Those characteristics of, and differences in, perception attributable more specifically to variations in meaning will be discussed in the following chapter.

6 Appraisive Aspects of the Image

Although vision is the dominant sensory mode, perception of, and resultant images of, the urban environment are more than a response to physical form. The latter is certainly emphasised in the specialised perception of the enquiring aesthete or visitor (for example Pocock, 1975), although it is questionable whether a pure aesthetic appreciation, devoid of emotional or symbolic content, is possible. Again, planners and architects may perceive the design element rather than social content of an area, thereby producing evaluations different from those of the residents. For Everyman, however, the designative aspects—size, shape, texture, disposition, etc. – may be less important *per se* than the appraisive – the meaning attaching to, or evoked by, the physical form.

If descriptive appraisal is considered part of the designative response, then the appraisive response to the environment may be divided into two components, the evaluative and the affective. The former is an assessment with two overlapping aspects: one of evaluation *per se*, an opinion or judgement, which may incorporate general or external standards but is without either obligatory comparison with other places or a particular behaviour objective; the second aspect, preference, specifically involves the assessing or ranking of a set of places according to a scale of preference. The affective component is concerned with the emotional reaction to place; it may be a response of the heart as much as of the mind, the realm of attitudes, feelings, beliefs.

In this chapter the evaluative component of the image will be examined first, and will include a degree of methodological orientation to illuminate the interpretation. The affective component will be tackled from a different viewpoint, with the deeper meaning of man's affective interrelation with environment being considered under the headings of the symbolism of place, sense of place, and the changing role of place.

EVALUATION OF THE ENVIRONMENT

The foundation of environmental evaluation is verbal description, whether by the use of free description, check list or rating according to a scale of 'betterness' or 'worseness'. On such foundations is based a whole range of analytical techniques of varying sophistication (see Craik, 1968). Whichever technique is used, however, it must be repeated that, given the multi-dimensional nature of the urban environment, its full features are unlikely to be revealed by a single technique, least of all a simple one.

A key problem in the identification of the elements of environmental assessment is the development of a lexicon of environmental descriptors which is meaningful, unambiguous, comprehensive and flexible in operation (Kasmar, 1970). The method of compilation is generally by means of a literature scan, pre-test questionnaire and use of a thesaurus. Each new work is therefore a potential contributor in the search for key dimensions, although at the moment literature reveals a general lack of comparability in descriptors at all levels, from those of landscape evaluation to those of room description (Craik, 1971). Two particular techniques, however, often used with principal components or factor analytic methods, which have given a boost to the process are the semantic differential and repertory grid approaches. The former was developed in psychology to measure word meaning (Osgood *et al.*, 1957). In its original context, the semantic differential technique postulates that meaning can be mapped into a three-dimensional spatial model, in which the dimensions are mutually orthogonal. However, as used by geographers in studying environmental images, 'semantic differential' studies are in general more accurately described as principal axis factor analyses of rating scale matrices. In any case, both the original and modified forms still require prior selection of descriptors. Repertory grid methods, however, originating this time in clinical psychology (Kelly, 1955) to elicit the personal construing of the world, have an added advantage over the semantic differential (Donnelly and Menzies, 1973, pp. 12–16) in that there is no required preselection of either concepts (elements) or descriptors (constructs). The ramifications of this, together with the whole question of image measurement, was discussed in chapter 4, a knowledge of which will be assumed in the following survey which illustrates the nature of environmental assessment at various levels of resolution.

A comparative assessment of four American cities–New York, Boston, Columbus, Cambridge – by the use of free description, selection of significant attributes and rating 25 bipolar attributes, showed a strong correlation between all three methods (Lowenthal, 1972). Table 6.1, listing the leading five attributes selected as most significant for each city, illustrates the varying degree of consensus among the four cities. Generally, environments evoking the strongest feeling – New York, in particular, and Boston – projected the most definite and consensal images. In contrast, those evoking little feeling projected relatively vague and neutral images, with much lower consensus of agreement. Among the different participant groups it was found that styles of environmental assessment changed with increasing age and formal education, becoming less emotional, more objective and less negative.

TABLE 6.1

FIVE MOST SIGNIFICANT ATTRIBUTES FOR FOUR AMERICAN CITIES

New York	%	*Boston*	%	*Columbus*	%	*Cambridge*	%
Rich	4.7	Business use	6.4	Living use	5.6	Contrast	5.1
Moving	6.7	Urban	5.6	Old	5.4	Interesting	4.5
Urban	5.4	Moving	4.9	Contrast	4.8	Pleasant	4.3
Interesting	5.4	Old	4.9	Pleasant	4.7	Old	4.0
Business use	4.7	Noisy	4.4	Interesting	4.3	Dense	3.6
Total per cent	28.9		26.2		24.8		21.5

Source: Lowenthal (1972), p. 13.

The structure of environmental attitudes in a study of residential preference among New Zealand towns (Jackson and Johnston, 1972) revealed four underlying dimensions. In fact eight dimensions had been hypothesised, measurable by 38 descriptors, using the semantic differential technique, but a principal components analysis of the data yielded only four meaningful components. The four components, accounting for 70 per cent of the original variance, were socio-economic quality, social and housing environments, climate and physical environment with special reference to greenness. Another general finding was that respondents held more precise and discriminating images of their home town compared to other centres.

The measurement of meaning with a minimum of interviewer influence by the use of the repertory grid method is well illustrated in a study of the image of Bath (Harrison and Sarre, 1975). Here again, it is interesting to compare the hypothesised structure of environmental meaning, as suggested by the distribution of the supplied constructs, with the actual elicited results (table 6.2 – the elements construed were 'places' considered 'important in everyday life' by a sample of middle-class housewives). The evaluative and affective components, far from accounting for over half the pattern, formed under one-quarter of the constructs proffered and only 15 per cent of the total used. The bulk was formed by descriptive and relational constructs, the latter describing how the individual comes into contact with the place and/or the role played by each.

TABLE 6.2

CLASSES OF CONSTRUCTS IN IMAGE STUDY OF BATH

Class	*Supplied to respondents*	*Chosen by respondents*	*Total uses by respondents*
Evaluative	4	15	30
Affective	1	2	3
Relational	3	33	86
Descriptive	1	23	49
Total	9	73	168

Source: Harrison and Sarre (1975), pp. 10–11.

The resultant spatial image, of an evaluative as opposed to designative nature, is shown in figure 6.1. The maps are derived from a principal component analysis of the element 'supergrid', that is the matrix composed of the common constructs (9) and total different places (745) supplied by respondents. The first component (figure 6.1b), accounting for 32.8 per cent of the variance, contrasts places which were liked and beautiful (the Georgian areas, especially Pulteney Street and The Circus – Camden Crescent; Botanical Gardens) with those which were disliked and ugly (mainly the lower Avon valley with its industry, communications and some working-

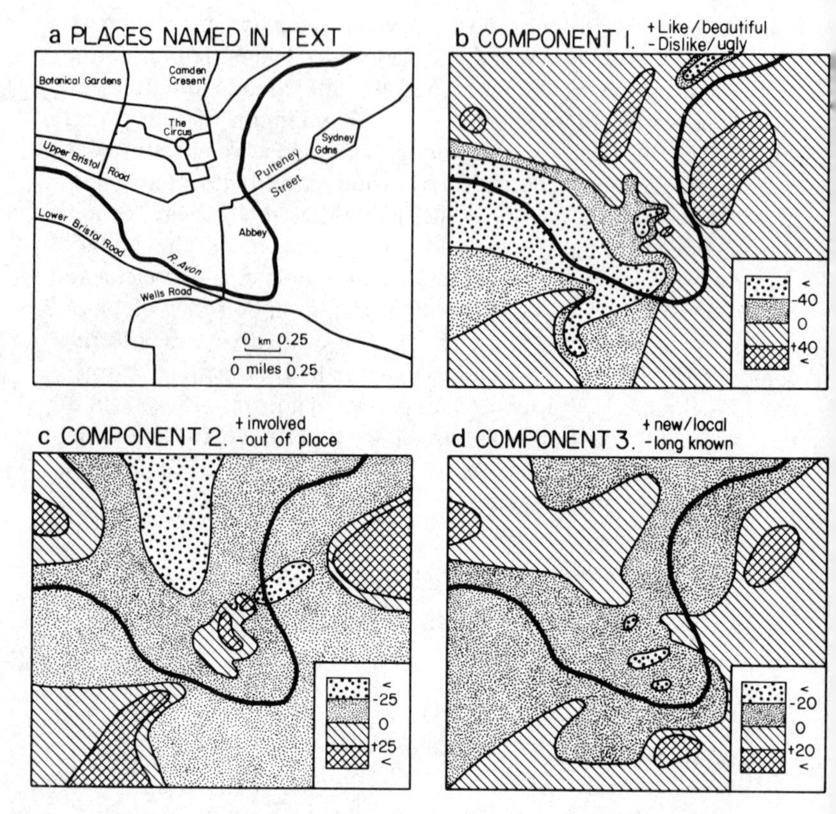

Figure 6.1 Images of Bath—spatial distribution of mean scores on leading components of element supergrid: a, Places mentioned in text; b, Component 1; c, Component 2; d, Component 3 (Source: Harrison and Sarre, 1975, p. 26)

class housing; plus Wells Road). The second component (figure 6.1c), accounting for 15.2 per cent of the variance, contrasts places in which respondents were involved (city centre and three middle-class residential areas) with those where the respondents felt out of place (notably the Georgian areas), being, perhaps, an example in terms of de Lauwe's levels of social space, where the respondents' aspiration level is above that of behaviour (see Buttimer, 1969). The third component (figure 6.1d), accounting for a further 12 per cent, distinguishes places known for a long time and of wide signficance (city centre) from places recently discovered and of local significance (some suburbs; Sydney Gardens; other places beyond the obviously known high spots). The structural and spatial characteristics of the components thus derived permitted the authors to speculate on the underlying behavioural processes (Harrison and Sarre, 1975, pp. 27–9), a step which the mapping of designative aspects hardly permits.

At the neighbourhood level an early use of adjectival descriptors was in Greensboro and Durham, North Carolina, where photographs were the stimulus to elicit the ideal environmental qualities for a residential area (Wilson, 1962). Of the 15 attributes, the most important were beauty, exclusiveness, spaciousness and a country-like character. (Interestingly, the respondents' own, as opposed to the ideal, neighbourhood emphasised social elements rather than physical ones.) The desirable visual quality of neighbourhoods in the Chicago metropolitan area, based on the rating of nine variables for a series of photographs, revealed a similar pattern (Peterson, 1967). The two outstanding dimensions were 'physical quality', associated with age and expensiveness, and 'harmony with nature', associated with greenness, privacy, open space and closeness to nature.

Studies using the preference approach to places reveal a general consensus in patterns of residential desirability, whether at the intra-urban level, for example Swansea (Herbert, 1973), Christchurch (Johnston, 1971); or the regional level, for example South Hampshire (Bateman *et al.*, 1974) or national level, for example within England (Goddard, 1971*b*), USA (Doherty, 1968), New Zealand (Johnston, 1970). Such studies, however, raise the question of the validity of isolating the concept of residential desirability from the totality or multi-dimensional nature of assessment. In general, the preferential ordering of areas by residential desirability and perceived social status shows a high positive correlation. Thus some behavioural studies of actual residential mobility – in which a distinct spatial bias is a common finding – discuss such mobility patterns in relation to mental maps, which are determined by the individuals' acitvity space (Horton and Reynolds, 1971). In many studies, however, this link is assumed – even, for instance, in the frequently quoted study of directional bias in Minneapolis, with its discussion of sectorally-biased mental maps (Adams, 1969).

Residential choice was linked to environmental preference in a study in South Hampshire and West Sussex (Bateman *et al.*, 1974). This work is of interest in that it is one of the few concerned with in-migrants, residential relocation being set within the broader survey of

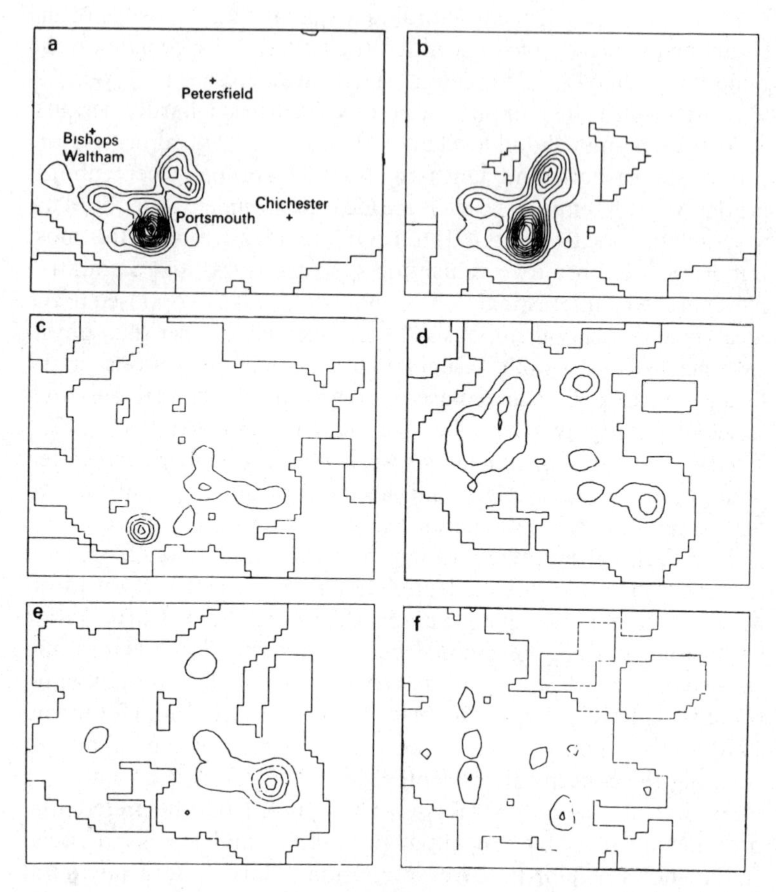

Figure 6.2 The pattern of residential preference in South Hampshire and West Sussex among indigenous and in-migrant office employees: a, Negative preference surface, indigenous group; b, Negative preference surface, in-migrants; c, Positive preference surface, indigenous group; d, Positive preference surface, in-migrants; e, Positive preference surface, high status in-migrants; f, Positive preference surface, low status in-migrants. A weighting ratio of 2.0: 1.5: 1.0 was used for the respondent's three ranked places; values were then transferred to a grid of one kilometre squares, from which a running mean of nine squares was used to generate the contours (Source: Bateman *et al.*, 1974, pp. 151–3)

the transfer of the headquarters of a major company from Central London to Portsmouth. Maps of residential preference were constructed from the migrants' selection and ranking of three places which most appealed, and the three most disliked, as 'potential areas in which to live'. The findings were compared with a local control group whose characteristics approximated those of the incoming group (figure 6.2).

For both groups the negative preference surface, indicating areas of dislike, is concentrated into a single 'mountain' centred near the actual place of work, whereas the positive preference surface shows a series of peaks (figure 6.2 a – d). The positive preference patterns are distinguished by the indigenous group indicating high attraction in part of Portsmouth, whereas the highest peak of appeal for newcomers is the historic cathedral town of Chichester, with highs in other small market towns (for example Petersfield) and villages. The areas thus highlighted, however, are a regional example of 'aspiration space' – previously illustrated in the study of Bath – for little correlation was shown with those areas where the majority actually chose to reside. The preferred surface among in-migrants varied, anyway, when socio-economic differences were considered. Disaggregation by status, for example, shows that the high status group are more oriented to rural and small town locations, whereas the low status group express a preference for outer suburb locations (figure 6.2 e – f).

In summary, the deduction of residential – or any other – preference pattern from behaviour can be a dangerous exercise in that people act not only on the basis of different sets of information (Pred, 1967), but also on different sets of criteria. Conversely, it is as well to reflect that behaviour, when reality is confronted, may bear little relation to evaluations or preferences previously expressed by the same individuals about hypothetical, ideal or even context-specific situations. Rather it is the case that behaviour reflects spatial and social constraints imposed on such people.

Preference within the retail environment was an early element in the so-called behavioural revolution in geography (see Huff, 1960), and owed much to image studies in the field of retail marketing, but detailed studies of cognitive evaluation are a later feature. One such study is that of the city centre in Bristol, using the semantic differential (Downs, 1970*a*). Nine 'cognitive categories', each measured by four bipolar adjectival scales, were the author's hypothesised dimensions by which shoppers evaluated the distinctive central area. Factor analysis confirmed six of the nine categories as distinctive dimensions, price, range of goods, visual appearance, service, structure and design, shopping hours. Of the remaining categories, 'ease of movement and internal parking' was divided into two separate dimensions, but 'reputation' and 'atmosphere' were distributed across many of the factors such that 'it might be argued that they do not exist' (Downs, 1970*a*, p. 36).

The same study of Bristol showed that consumers did not hold generalised images of centres lower in the shopping hierarchy, only perceptions of individual shops within the particular centres. Hudson (1974) went on to investigate images of individual food shops in Bristol, using the repertory grid method. Price levels and distance from the respondents' homes were found to be the most common and important dimensions of the shop image. At the same level of resolution, Garner (1968) used the semantic differential to illustrate the different images held of women's clothes shops, again in Bristol. Here 29 scales were rated and a comparison of similarity profiles suggested a threefold grouping: national chains of good reputation, boutiques with inexpensive merchandise, and shops with conservative-style merchandise. In a rare study of the evaluation of the retail environment from the point of view of the shopkeeper, rather than consumer, Harrison and Sarre (1975) used repertory grids and distilled three distinct components from these – one descriptive of the physical nature of the environment, another relating to the running of the shop, and the third an evaluative bipolar split between objective and subjective elements.

Towards the lower end of the spatial scale Herschberger (1972), reviewing research work in architectural psychology in America and Britain, confidently reported having established at least a beginning towards a definitive set of semantic scales to measure the meaning of architectural environments. Six major factors were distinguished. They are listed, with the representative descriptor scales, in table 6.3. It can be seen that, after the leading two factors, the response is of descriptive appraisal – 'representational' rather than 'responsive' in Herschberger's terms – a characteristic increasingly emphasised if his further 14 minor factors are considered. One point concerning work at this scale of environmental assessment in view of its practical application, is the reported similarity between the semantic dimensions used by architects and non-architects. Once more, however, it should be pointed out that the groups chosen to represent the latter are typically articulate and educated samples (Canter and Wools, 1970; Herschberger, 1968).

TABLE 6.3

LEADING FACTORS, WITH SEMANTIC DESCRIPTOR SCALES, IN EVALUATION OF ARCHITECTURAL ENVIRONMENTS

Factor		*Descriptor scale*
1	Aesthetic	Unique – Common
2	Friendliness	Friendly – Hostile
3	Organisation	Ordered – Chaotic
4	Potency	Rugged – Delicate
5	Space	Loose – Compact
6	Ornate	Ornate – Plain

Source: Herschberger (1972), 6–4–9.

The above illustrations suggest that, although evaluation is a personal response, underlying consistencies can be found. The overwhelming reliance on verbal techniques, however, assumes that people can articulate their perceptions. Here, quite apart from interpersonal variation rooted in cultural and/or class differences, there remains the fundamental point that semantic responses can capture only a fraction of what man perceives in the environment: however sophisticated the technique, there will always remain those thoughts which, even for the poet, 'lie too deep for tears'. The treatment of the specifically affective component of the image in the following sections will, therefore, differ from that above, in that attention will be turned more directly to the environment to explore the emotional value and symbolic importance of place to man.

CITY AS SYMBOL

Physical features of the environment achieve significance or imageability through association with a particular activity or function, or, more generally and in a more subtle manner, through the adherence of particular sentiments, memories, attitudes or beliefs. The city, for instance, is clearly more than bricks and mortar, more than a utility for living; it is the visible expression of man's value system – his beliefs, ideals, hopes and fears – the supreme expression of civilisation (Mumford, 1961). 'Men may find God in nature, but when they look at cities they are viewing themselves,' writes Ylivsaker (1971, p. 7), echoing the poet Cowper two hundred years previously. The city was neither built, nor is it experienced, as an exercise in pure form. Physical form mediates a higher form, suggesting or symbolising ideas and properties not necessarily obvious or inherent in the objects themselves. This may be illustrated with reference to both over-all form and detailed structure.

In the ancient city commerce, defence and irrigation imperatives have been interpreted as 'no more than external parametric conditions' (Wheatley, 1971, p. 477); the form is explicable in cosmo-religious terms, with man attempting to produce a territorial version of the cosmological ideal (Bogdanovic, 1975; Smith, 1974*c*). Perfection was symbolised in a regular geometrical outline, usually a circle or square. The function of the surrounding wall, antedating any defence role, was to enclose the sacred, habitable space from the profane, inferior, the sub-urban. Within the area delimited as sacred, the main intersecting axes were oriented to the cardinal points east – west (direction of sunrise and sunset, or of birth and death) and north – south (symbolising cold and warmth), thereby producing the four 'quarters', the name still given to city districts, however many in number. Such axiality helped to achieve centripetality, focusing on one quintessentially sacred point, the location for temple or palace. At this point were the tallest buildings, the vertical symbols of cosmological significance pointing up to heaven – the ziggurat, tower, dome or spire. Here contact with the supernatural was possible; from this point temporal power flowed outwards along the main axes to the four corners of the earth through city gates ostentatiously large to symbolise this authority.

The cosmological or religious conception described above was lost in medieval market towns and in the industrial towns of the last century, although an over-all symbolic interpretation is valid for Renaissance cities, for the newly-planned capitals of the past two hundred years from L'Enfant's Washington to Costa's Brazilia, and for Howard's idea of Garden Cities and some of the British new towns subsequently built. More often, however, one particular construction or landmark is the supreme symbol of the present city. Within the city important individual buildings have always been public symbols proclaiming through the classic language of architecture messages of power, order, glory, freedom (Summerson, 1964). The phenomenal absolutism and cultural symbolism inherent in such classic language, however, were debased in the industrial town, where dome and pediment could now signify the gaol or museum or 'anything else', as Dickens (1854, chapter 5) observed of Coketown. Stained glass has now descended to semi's in suburbia, where also lawn and garden can be interpreted as symbolising meadow and field, with pets the substitute for livestock (Tuan, 1974*a*, p. 237).

A social hierarchy is no longer observed among buildings. The most prominent constructions are rarely concerned with ecclesiastical or civil administration, but are, rather, office blocks, factories, multi-storey car parks, or even feats of motorway engineering. Symbols of successful materialism and economic competitiveness now dominate the skyline. Witness the 'leap-frogging' nature of the competition within and between American cities where the tallest block is successively exceeded by the latest, momentary symbol of economic success. In Britain during the 1960s there was similar emulation among municipal authorities to erect towering multi-storey residential blocks, monuments to their respective department's technical proficiency although flying in the face of economic and sociological realities. At ground level the assault on the senses of the American franchise strip (Venturi *et al.*, 1973) represents an apex of commercialism, with the car the supreme symbol of this 'drive-in' world such that its deprivation has been deemed tantamount to emasculation (Rudofsky, 1969. p. 342).

Below the level of monumental architecture, the city is still rife with symbolism. In G.K. Chesterton's words,

> The city is, properly speaking, more poetic even than a countryside . . . there is no stone in the street and no brick in the wall that is not actually a deliberate symbol — a message from some man, as much as if it were a telegram or a postcard. The narrowest street possesses, in every nook and twist of its intention, the soul of the man who built it, perhaps long in his grave. Every brick has as human a hieroglyph as if it were a graven brick of Babylon: every slate on the roof is as educational a document as if it were a slate covered with addition and subtraction sums.
>
> (G.K. Chesterton, 1901, pp. 158–9).

Of course, such appreciation requires eyes to perceive, but the house (Cooper, 1972; 1974), domestic neighbourhood or townscape, although perhaps not built as symbol, acquires meaning and thus becomes symbol. The green swards and privet, the gnomescapes, the graffiti are all condensed statements about the people who inhabit the areas, a reflection of individual and collective values. Their creation is an extension of the residents' identity; their continued existence provides a symbol of security and stability in a changing world. With the passage of time elements are raised beyond any intrinsic merit through their association with life's events, such that they provide a 'contextual environment' able to reactivate memories for the individual or group (Smith, 1974*a*). The concepts of 'mythicised' place (Raban, 1974) or of 'associative power' of place (Lenz-Romeiss, 1973) incorporate identical reasoning. As the scene for particular social activity, the environment becomes associated in the mind with, and therefore symbolic of, that activity. Thus, in time, although the physical structure is seen, the response is to its social meaning. The response is therefore symbolic – not to what *is*, but to what it *represents* – that is, to the sense of place.

SENSE OF PLACE

> Every continent has its own great spirit of place. Every people is polarised in some particular locality, which is home, the homeland. Different places on the face of the earth have different vital effluence, different vibration, different chemical exhalation, different polarity with different stars: call it what you like. But the spirit of place is a great reality.
>
> (Lawrence, 1924, p. 12).

Spirit or sense of place is concerned with the relations between place and person, an awareness of the distinctive character of specific localities (Briggs, 1970). The concept, however, is a broad one and incorporates aspects of imageability, topophilia (see Tuan, 1974*a*), attachment and the symbolic meaning of places. Two dimensions are recognisable, a physical and a social – psychological.

The strength of the physical image derives from the distinctive combination of local topography and built form. The ease of recognition and recollection of a pen – picture or symbolic image is a ready measure of such distinctiveness. The absence of such a quick recall may well indicate a certain place*less*ness. As Gertrude Stein is said to have remarked of Oakland, California, 'When you get there, there's no there, there' (Chermayeff and Alexander, 1966, p. 50). One of Lynch's (1960, p. 41) respondents referred to Los Angeles in similar terms.

Although there are, apparently, times when it is 'better to travel than to arrive', it says little for the end-points, since place is initially distinguished from space by external bounding and internal structuring, such that there is a recognisable 'insideness' and 'outsideness'. A sense of place, however, comes from the further attribution of meaning to such physical form, the third stage in place-making which Rapoport (1972) calls 'personalisation'. There is, therefore, a social or psychological interaction, a reciprocal relationship between place and person.

Place is clearly affected by people; as the individual personality is reflected in home and possessions, so collective personality and values are translated into the wider environment or 'cultural' landscapes (Lowenthal and Prince, 1964; 1965). On the other hand, people are affected by place. Witness, for instance, the contrast in attitudes adopted in different public places – a cathedral, sports stadium, waiting room, rail compartment.

The influence of the built environment, however, is not one of simple causality, but rather as one cause or influence among several (Broady, 1968; Lee, 1971). The arrangement of furniture in a room, or rooms within a building, or buildings within a neighbourhood clearly do affect man's response and behaviour. To deny this would be to negate the validity of the design professions and the recent injection of architectural psychology (Canter, 1974; Lang *et al.*, 1974; Sommer, 1969; 1972). The influence, however, is reciprocal: the well-known utterance of Sir Winston Churchill that 'we shape our buildings, and afterwards our buildings shape us' (Merton, 1948, p. 204), summarises this process. Churchill was speaking in favour of an identical rebuilding of the House of Commons chambers despite their acknowledged inadequate size, the argument being that parliamentary debates had been conditioned by the physical character of the old House, and that to change this would affect the manner of debate and hence the very structure of British democracy.

There is, therefore, an interaction *with*, rather than response *to*, place, in effect a sense of relatedness. The nature of this relatedness amid rural scenes is described vividly in the poetry of Wordsworth.

To him the 'spirit of place' – a phrase used in *The Prelude* – required 'a heart that watches and receives', for the personality, unlike skin-deep appearance, is not revealed on brief acquaintance. In this respect, people are no different from places. Hence Tuan's phrase (1974*b*) of places being 'fields of care' Langer (1953, p. 95), in a discussion of virtual space, had earlier used similar terms when describing place in a non-geographical sense as being 'a created thing, an ethnic domain made visible, tangible, sensible'. Interaction with the associative power of place is of a symbolic nature; to be among the initiate one must be able to read such symbolic language. Time is therefore an important component of sense of place.

Time deepens the relatedness of person and endows place with a patina of meaning. Its importance in the environment can be readily illustrated – in the positive relationship between age and veneration, regardless or architectural merit; in the preference for restoration rather than the replica, however drastic the restorative action; in the public reaction to threatened historic buildings, regardless of whether they are frequently visited; in the chagrin of the new owners which drove them to artificially replace the grime which the clean air of Arizona stripped from the recontructed London bridge.

Places need a legibility of time and change, a sense of when-ness as well as whereness (Lynch, 1972). Atemporal environments, those with no definable allegiance to any particular period and lacking a sense of continuity, are uncomfortable environments (for example, Lurie, 1966). People, in turn, need a depth of acquaintance for, as Lowenthal (1975) argues, only through our memories, and that of others, do we truly understand any scene. The effect of the lack of any such acquaintance or 'preparedness' is illustrated in the collective reaction of Pasternak's rail travellers who, finding themselves, because of a suicide suddenly halted at an unknown location,

> felt as if the whole place had only been brought into being by the halt, and that neither the squelchy marsh nor broad river nor the fine house and church on the steep bank opposite would have existed except for the accident. Even the sun . . . seemed to be a stage prop, a purely local manifestation.
>
> (Pasternak, 1958, chapter 1).

The stability and continuity of an enduring environment is also effective therapy against the general rapidity and scale of modern social and environmental changes, the current rate of which has planning and policy implications for sense of place. In brief, can one preserve or create a sense of place? (Goodey, 1974*c*). Conservation areas are already designated, and individual buildings scheduled for preservation, by architects; areas of natural beauty or interest are preserved on the advice of ecologists; the obvious omission is a social – psychological input. What constitutes a community? What is the hierarchy of life's social spaces and what is the implication of their spatial correlates for a sense of relatedness?

Work at the local level has shown the urban neighbourhood – once the confusion of definition and types has been clarified (Blowers, 1973) – to be a socio-spatial phenomenon (Lee, 1968), with people building up a mental model or schema of the area, territorially and not density-based, in which daily lives are played out. From the middle 1960s there have been official surveys into community attitudes including 'home area', national programmes giving priorities to inner city areas and government policy turning from redevelopment to rehabilitation (see Lee, 1975). At a different scale, American cities have been said to be ungovernable because their excessive size prohibits a sense of place or belonging: people are no longer 'citizens', caring and relating to their city, but merely inhabitants (Goodman, 1969). Identity may be lost, therefore, beyond critical thresholds. It is well known that overpatronage of tourist centres may cause deterioration to the physical environment; an excess of visitors is also deleterious to the more intangible sense of place, the very uniqueness which makes a centre a tourist attraction in the first instance.

Size threshold is clearly critical in any attempt to create a sense of place. A more fundamental question, however, is whether a variety of meaningful sensory experiences can be implanted when it is the values which people come to vest in the area that constitute the intangible ethos or feeling. This is a process which involves the passage of time. From a behavioural point of view, the planner can only provide the equivalent of what Gans (1972) calls a 'potential environment', having regard to the client group and his own elitist position, a topic which will be developed further in chapter 9.

CHANGING ROLE OF PLACE

If discussion of relatedness turns more specifically from identification *of* to identification *with* place, then a changing role can be seen in which the need for a sense of place has been queried.

Formerly, society was highly localised, structured and self-contained, with the city wall the visual symbol of confinement. In the world we have lost, everything physical was on the human scale, with no built object bigger than London Bridge or St Paul's cathedral, and everything temporal was tied to the human life-span (Laslett, 1968). In the world we have gained society is characterised by its mobility–social, spatial and mental. The mind has been blown open: all the world's the stage in this electronic era and available in any lounge at the turn of a switch. Messages are no longer confined to the range of eye vision or inter-personal communication; 'reference groups' on which the behaviour of society is modelled are increasingly national rather than local. In the realm of transport, the aeroplane offers 'earth shrinkers' and the railway 'brings places nearer', but it is the motor car which is the supreme 'escape machine' for 'getaway people'.

The confines of localised place have therefore been overcome. As a consequence the traditional community has been replaced by an interest-based 'communality' (McClenahan, 1945) or 'non-place urban realm' (Webber, 1964*a*,*b*). In Webber's words, 'it is interaction, not place, that is the essence of the city and city life' (Webber, 1964*a*, p. 116). Cox (1965) introduced the term 'technopolitan man' with a culture distinct from 'tribal' and even 'urban man', enjoying freedom, anonymity and maximum choice within the modern technopolis.

Mobility, mass media, mass production, mass culture — in brief, modern technology — have lessened place distinctiveness and, apparently, man's reliance on place. Mobility and release from place might be taken therefore as a sign of advanced, civilised man. By deduction, then, current reliance on place and place distinctiveness in advanced societies may be interpreted as a sign of backwardness and symptom of social deprivation. The last conclusion, however, has not been proven in empirical case studies (for example Townsend and Taylor, 1975). Neither is the general underlying thesis fully convincing.

Place will remain important, in the first instance, through a unique relationship with one's birthplace; 'a certain part of our senses are rooted for ever to the locality in which . . . we first saw light' (Sillitoe, 1975, p. 59). Moreover, 'geopiety', a strong bond or reverence for the territorial home and homeland, has been shown to be an enduring characteristic of societies, both east and west (Tuan, 1976). The immediate physical and social environment is, without doubt, crucially important in the early psychological and social development of the individual.

Although differentiation of self is an important part in the very early development of the individual's identity, there remains the broader, philosophical question of the extent to which man is part of nature or place, or outside it. Primitive man viewed himself as an integral part of nature until the spread of Christianity in the western world stripped nature of its own spirits; only technopolitan man sees himself unequivocally above or outside it. To the philosopher it remains a false dichotomy to think of nature *and* man (see Tuan, 1971*b*). Man is part of nature or, in MacKinder's (1935, p. 9) colourful eloquence, 'man is a part of his own environment, as cheese-mites are a part of the cheese'. Durrell (1969, p. 163), a modern writer with particular sensitivity to the feel of places, describes the symbiosis as man 'existing in nature, as a function of place'. Confirmation of this attitude is found among those disoriented by the pace of current environmental change.

As local geographies are razed in redevelopment and relocation schemes, the psychological reaction of those involved is grief and fragmentation of the sense of 'spatial identity' (Fried, 1963). It is not only the built environment that is razed but also the contextual environment, the symbol of life's experiences: part of people's roots, part of *themselves*, is lost. This process is highlighted in the poetry of John Clare, who lost his sense of place and identity—and, ultimately, his sanity—from the dislocation wrought by parliamentary enclosure of the open fields around his village of Helpston, Lincolnshire (Barrell, 1972). The psychiatrist is to be heeded, then, when he writes that

> there is, within the human individual, a sense of *relatedness to his total environment* . . . and that if he tries to ignore its importance to himself, he does so at the peril of his psychological well-being
> (Searles, 1961, p. 31).

Moreover, if the evolution of human behaviour and mental satisfaction is approached, and parallels sought, through the study of animal behaviour a key concept of territoriality emerges. Ethologists have shown that, equal in importance to basic physical drives, are three psychological needs — identity, security and stimulation — for which territory is essential (Ardrey, 1967; Lorenz, 1966; Morris, 1969). There is, then, a consensus among authors that an optimum relation with place is essential to mental well-being and development of identity, and that a sense of place is a reinforcement of identity — even an extension of, or integral part of, man's identity.

Place is also important to the modern car-owning community in that mobility presupposes a structured image and base from which to explore or 'use' the city. This is explicit from Lynch's (1960, p. 124) early work, where the function of the environmental image was to permit 'purposeful mobility', and from the dual nature of the element place in Norberg-Schulz's classification, where places were described as 'foci where we experience the meaningful events of our existence... also points of departure from which we orient ourselves and take possession of the environment' (Norberg-Schulz, 1971, p. 19). It is surely not coincidence, therefore, to find the mobile middle class behind the recent boom in locality-based interest groups concerned with historical, ecological or amenity qualities of place. Or to find that as standardisation and centralisation increase in administrative and economic spheres, conforming to spatial – economic realities, there is a general awakening of regional and environmental consciousness. Mobile man is apparently wishing – or needing – to relate more genuinely to local and regional distinctiveness.

The non car-owning sections of society necessarily remain place-bound communities. Thus, for a sizeable section of society, the young, old, and poor, the relationship to place remains intimate and restricted. Moreover, since increasing middle-class mobility may be detrimental to these disadvantaged groups, by further limiting their mobility through the contraction of public transport, it remains dangerous to generalise about the mobile society. For all of these reasons, therefore, one may conclude that 'mobility will never destroy the importance of locality' (Pahl, 1968, p. 48). The appraisive or symbolic content of, and response to, place are crucial to man's existence.

7 Environmental Images and Learning

In the context of environmental images, learning necessitates consideration of the development of environmental images, of the build-up of knowledge and meaning of place and space. The issues of learning and change in images, however, have been relatively neglected, a condition attributable to three main factors. First are the problems of measuring the image at one point in time and the consequent channelling of effort and resources to that end. Second are the conceptual and, perhaps even more vital, operational problems associated with studying change in environmental images. The most appropriate way to study such change would be via longitudinal studies, thus monitoring change in the image over time. Such a research strategy poses severe problems and usually neccessitates the adoption of an alternative strategy, a cross-sectional strategy based upon attempting to infer learning from the differences in the content and structure of images held by different groups at one point in time. This alternative approach, in turn, raises serious inferential problems. The third main reason for the neglect of learning in studies of environmental images is that, while there are a variety of theories of learning developed in psychology, these are not wholly appropriate as a conceptual framework for studying changing environmental images.

This problem is particularly marked in the case of stimulus – response learning theories in which learning is defined as a change in behaviour rather than as a change in environmental images. But even the adoption of those approaches in which learning is defined as cognitive rather than behavioural change raises problems. Such theories – as those of Lewin or Tolman – often lack suitable operational definitions of their theoretical concepts. In particular, methods of measuring the image are usually not specified (see chapter 2).

Moreover, in general, learning theories in psychology have been developed on a different scale in relation to different problems, often in the context of laboratory animal experiments, rather than with macro-scale problems of spatial learning and the development of environmental images. Such theories contain little that is explicitly addressed to spatial learning and must be reinterpreted in terms of spatial and environmental learning (although there are exceptions, mentioned in chapter 2).

There is, however, one approach to learning originating in psychology that is of considerable utility in studying learning as it relates to environmental images. This involves theories and studies of the child's development of spatial concepts and knowledge, and the first part of the remainder of this chapter is devoted to this topic. Following from this, some consideration is given to the sources of knowledge that contribute to the development of environmental images: primary sources, such as search and habitual behaviour in the environment; and secondary sources, such as the mass media, television and radio, films, newspapers, literature and the printed word in its various forms.

DEVELOPMENT OF CHILDREN'S CONCEPTS AND KNOWLEDGE OF SPACE

It is useful to distinguish between theories of cognitive development in children and empirical studies of the child's development of spatial concepts and knowledge that draw upon these. Likewise, distinctions can be drawn between learning (a quantitative change in amounts of knowledge) and development (a qualitative change in the organisation of behaviour). There are a number of theories of cognitive development (in a general sense) in children, notably that of Piaget, and more specific theories of the development of spatial concepts (for an extended review of these see Hart and Moore, 1973). Such theories are primarily concerned with concepts of the form and structure of space rather than the meaning of space; that is, with designative rather than appraisive aspects of the image of space. Two such theories are briefly considered here: those of Werner and Piaget.

Werner's (1957) organismic – developmental theory of space sees the child's cognitive development proceeding through three developmental progressions. The first of these is progressive self – object differentiation, during which the child learns to differentiate himself from the surrounding environment. This is usually attained by the age of two years. Following this, the second phase is one of progressive constructivism, usually completed by the age of eight, when the child becomes increasingly active and begins to construct its own image of the world. The third phase is constructive perspectivism, characterised by the ability of the child to adopt other people's viewpoints.

Paralleling these three developmental progressions, Werner sees three levels of development – sensorimotor, perceptual and contemplative – and three types of spatial experience – action in space, perception of space and conception of space. Therefore, Werner derives a specific theory of the development of notions of space, based on his more general developmental theory. The development of notions of space is seen as a process involving the increasing differentiation of the child and environment, followed by a reintegration between the self and environment. This is shared in a general way with Piaget, whose equilibration theory of the development of the child's conception of space posits cognitive development to be a result of interactions between the child and the environment. (For the best introduction to this work see Piaget, 1968.) Knowledge is thus constructed; interaction between person and environment leads to the attainment of an equilibrium. The rationale for development is adaptation: adaptation is the equilibration of assimilation and accommodation, assimilation being the taking in of knowledge about the outside world, accommodation the adjustment of existing ideas about the world in the light of this knowledge.

Piaget not only identifies four periods of development (in contrast to Werner's three) but spells out the criteria on which these are founded. There are two general criteria which in turn imply four more specific ones. The general criteria are hierarchisation – that all stages come in a fixed order of succession – and equilibration – that each stage is a step in a developmental progression. These imply that there is qualitative differentiation, integration, consolidation and coordination between stages.

The four major periods of development identified on the basis of these criteria are sensorimotor, preoperational, concrete operations and formal operations. The sensorimotor period, generally completed by the age of two, marks a change from the 'passive' to 'active' child, capable of coordinated action and internalised thought. In the preoperational phase the child begins to represent the external world symbolically and operate mentally on these symbols. However, the child's view is at this stage egocentric. This phase, usually found from 5 to 9 years, is replaced by the phase of concrete operations which is typically attained between 9 and 13 years of age. The period of concrete operations sees the child as capable of logical thought. The forms of thought developed in the preoperational phase become highly stabilised equilibrations of what were previously intuitive patterns. The child is now capable of separating his own viewpoint from those of others. The concrete operational phase is succeeded by that of formal operations, from the age of about 13 onwards. The formal operational phase is characterised by the ability for reflective abstraction strictly in the realm of ideas, by the ability to think symbolically.

On the basis of this general theory of cognitive development, Piaget derives a specific theory of the development of conceptions of space. A number of points can be made in relation to this. First, representations of space arise from the coordination and internalisation of actions: that is, knowledge of space is a function of action rather than perception (in the sense of the psychologist's use of this term). Related to this, the genesis of images of space arises from the internalisation of deferred imitations: initially, the child copies other people's actions but later these become remembered and so available when appropriate at a later time. A third point is that there are four levels (or structures) of spatial organisation corresponding to the four major periods of development outlined above. Finally, there are three classes of specific spatial relations which form the content of spatial cognition: topological, which develop first; projective; metric or Euclidean.

Drawing together and summarising the main themes of the work of Werner and Piaget, two main points can be made. First, the child's conception of space is neither innate nor learned (in the sense of being an accumulation of knowledge). Rather, to borrow Piaget's terminology, conceptions of space are constructed as a series of hierarchically ordered equilibrations through adaptive interactions with the environment, via the reciprocating processes of assimilation and accommodation. From the internalisation and reflective abstraction of actions arises the child's first intuitive understanding of space. More generally, this perspective implies that cognitive development is more than the simple accumulation of fact. Second, there are several dimensions to the child's developing understanding of space. There is

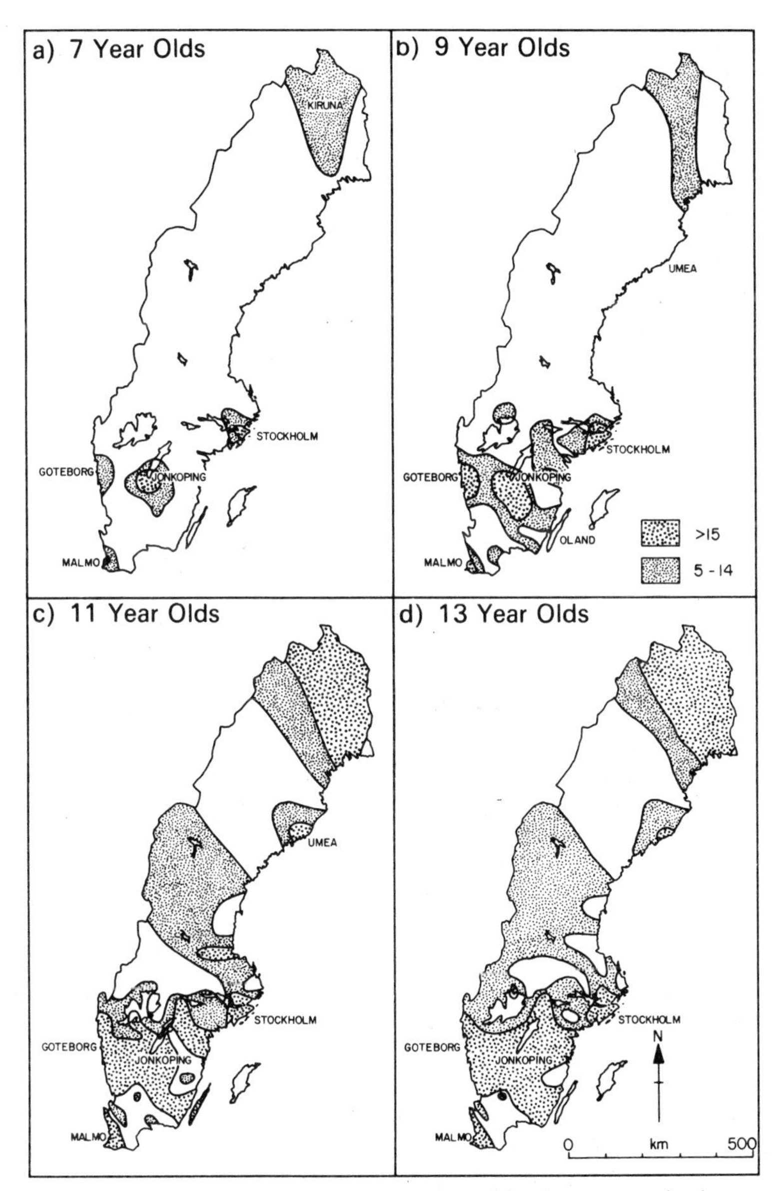

Figure 7.1 Growth in information surface of Sweden among schoolchildren of Jönköping (Source: Gould and White, 1974, pp. 134–8)

a progression from concrete to abstract notions of space: from sensorimotor action in space, to perceptions of space, to symbolic representations of space. Similarly, there is progression from a purely egocentric viewpoint to one which recognises a variety of possible perspectives.

It is against this background that the various studies of place and space learning and the development of spatial cognition in young children can be considered. Some of these (for example Blaut *et al.*, 1970; Ladd, 1970; 1972; Stea and Blaut, 1973*a,b*) can be interpreted against the theoretical background outlined above, others (Gould, 1973; Maurer and Baxter, 1972) cannot but are nevertheless of interest and will be dealt with first. Gould (1973) examined the knowledge of Sweden possessed by a number of schoolchildren in the town of Jonkoping in South-Central Sweden (figure 7.1). At the age of seven, children's knowledge was highly concentrated on their home town, with subsidiary peaks of knowledge centred on the major cities of Sweden – Stockholm, Goteborg and Malmo. At the age of nine, the children's information surface had both increased in depth and expanded in spatial extent. For example, the children had a fair degree of knowledge of Oland, an island that forms a major holiday centre for families in South Sweden. However, the four nodes that were dominant at seven remain dominant, and there is virtually no knowledge of North Sweden among nine year olds. But by the age of thirteen this is no longer so, for by this age the information surface has both risen and expanded and it appears that some sort of saturation level has been reached. Thus knowledge grows outward from the home area and develops unevenly over space as important places become known, while for many other areas, although they are known to a degree, levels of information remain low.

Maurer and Baxter (1972) studied children's images of their homes, neighbourhoods, journeys to school, city, and favourite and disliked places in Houston, Texas. Age had little effect on children's imagery, a rather surprising result as Maurer and Baxter were studying a group of 96 children aged between 7 and 14 years. The only significant difference between groups was that younger children drew a much less extensive map of the neighbourhood than did older children. This contrasts with the differences between age groups found by Gould (1973) and suggests that spatial scale is a pertinent consideration here. In contrast to age, however, the effect of race was very strong. White children's images were more extensive than those of black or Mexican American children while those of black children in particular emphasised the home. It was suggested that these differences reflected socio-economic factors such as migrational and travel mobility.

Other studies of children's learning can be more easily related to theoretical perspectives in developmental psychology. Despite the complex nature of 'place' as a stimulus, generally both too large to be perceived at one point in time and representing a complex array of people, objects and events, there is a certain amount of empirical evidence of place learning in young children. Further, much of this research has been carried out in a cross-cultural context. This evidence suggests that children of pre-school age can recognise places and solve mapping problems, for example simple route-finding exercises, prior to being introduced to 'formal' maps. Such children can interpret aerial photographs – iconic, non-linguistic maps – and read and use these as maps. This implies an ability to recognise and deal with the basic map properties of scale, projection and abstraction prior to formal instruction in the use of maps. Though there are variations in ability between children of differing socio-economic and environmental backgrounds, in general this ability is fully developed by the age of nine years. This raises questions as to the processes whereby these abilities and conceptions of space develop, as they do not depend on the formal educational process. It would seem that the critical factor, by which the child overcomes its limited perceptual and movement capacity to develop abstract conceptions of space, is that of toy-play. The child uses toys as models of elements of the 'real world' and by manipulating the position and relationship of these elements, develops the necessary conceptual apparatus to be able to correctly infer spatial relationships from aerial photographs. This supports the general proposition of concepts of space resulting from actions and interactions between the child and the environment.

The ability to develop cognitive maps of large-scale spatial environments (referred to as topographical representations by Hart and Moore, 1973), implies the development of a reference system both to relate the individual to the environment and elements of the environment to one another, and to organise the form and structure of the designative aspects of the environmental image. Developmentally, one can think of three orientational stages in such a reference system: first, an egocentric reference system, oriented with respect to the individual's actions; second, a fixed system of reference, oriented to a fixed location such as the child's home (which begins to introduce some notions of meaning and appraisive aspects to the development of the designative aspects of the image); third, a coordinated reference system, oriented to an abstract coordinate system, for example, lines of latitude and longitude.

Further, one can interpret this development of spatial reference systems in terms of Piaget's four levels of development of spatial concepts. In the sensorimotor phase, the child moves solely in a space of action, orientation to the environment is totally egocentric and there are no mental representations of space. The preoperational phase sees the beginnings of representational space. The internalisation of spatial behaviour leads to the child's first images or iconic representations of space. Spatial relationships are conceived topologically and the seeds of projective and metric relationships sown. Egocentric orientation is replaced by orientation with respect to definite locations: initially the home, later a small number of discontinuous and uncoordinated routes, landmarks and familiar places (which again implies the crucial role of meaning in this transition). In sum, these changes imply a gradual differentiation of the child from the environment, of the child's viewpoint from those of others, of environmental elements from their relationships. The phase of concrete operations sees the coordination of formerly discrete elements such as routes, landmarks and locations, into an organised whole. At the same time, geometric concepts such as angle and parallelism develop so that the child can now coordinate and construct a Euclidean (metric) frame of reference, which is critical in comprehending the large-scale environment. Finally, in the formal operations phase, characterised by reflective abstraction from concrete operations, the individual can contemplate a theoretical space abstracted from any concrete particulars (though this ability develops to varying degrees between people).

Therefore, it is clear that some important advances have been made in conceptualising the development of concepts of space in children and that these have served both to stimulate useful empirical research and provide a framework within which to interpret the results of this research. Generally, however, this work has concentrated on the form and structure of space, the designative aspects of the image. While this is important, the issues of the development of appraisive aspects of environmental images are largely ignored (though implicit in much of this work as has been pointed out).

SOURCES OF INFORMATION AND IMAGE FORMATION

While there is considerable evidence to suggest that man is basically curious, actively, though selectively, seeking information about his environment (Berlyne, 1962; 1963; Kelly, 1955), there are limits to his capacity to search and seek out information. Within the universe of information that, in principle, is available, people vary in their acquiring and processing abilities (Pred, 1967). In part this reflects the differential impact of those constraints that limits information acquisiton. Constraints are imposed by the time and money costs involved in seeking information, especially where these involve travel, but such costs affect different people to differing degrees. Other constraints relate to the alternative purposes for which resources used in search could be used. However, the costs committed to information acquisition must be balanced against the value or importance of the desired information.

Recognising the existence of such costs, one can identify two main types of information source that contribute to the development of environmental images: primary and secondary. Primary sources of information involve direct contact with the environment, in contrast to secondary sources where information is acquired second-hand and relates both to places visited and not visited (see figure 7.2). The importance of direct contact with the environment and interaction between self and environment in the formation of conceptions of space in young children has already been pointed out. Direct contact with the environment remains a potent source of knowledge in later life. But given the importance of travel and moving over space in acquiring environmental information, the inhibitory effects of travel cost, for long a central concern of human geographers, are important in influencing both those areas known and the depth of knowledge of these areas via information acquired in this way. Historically, however, it is important to remember that the cost of travel has, on average, declined. People are more mobile and their direct contact with the environment has extended over greater areas. For example, the recent rise in mass tourism, originating from the industrialised countries, has extended many people's experience of foreign countries, albeit in a partial and selective manner (Young, 1973).

In general, the volume of trip-making declines with distance from trip origins but is positively related to the perceived attraction of

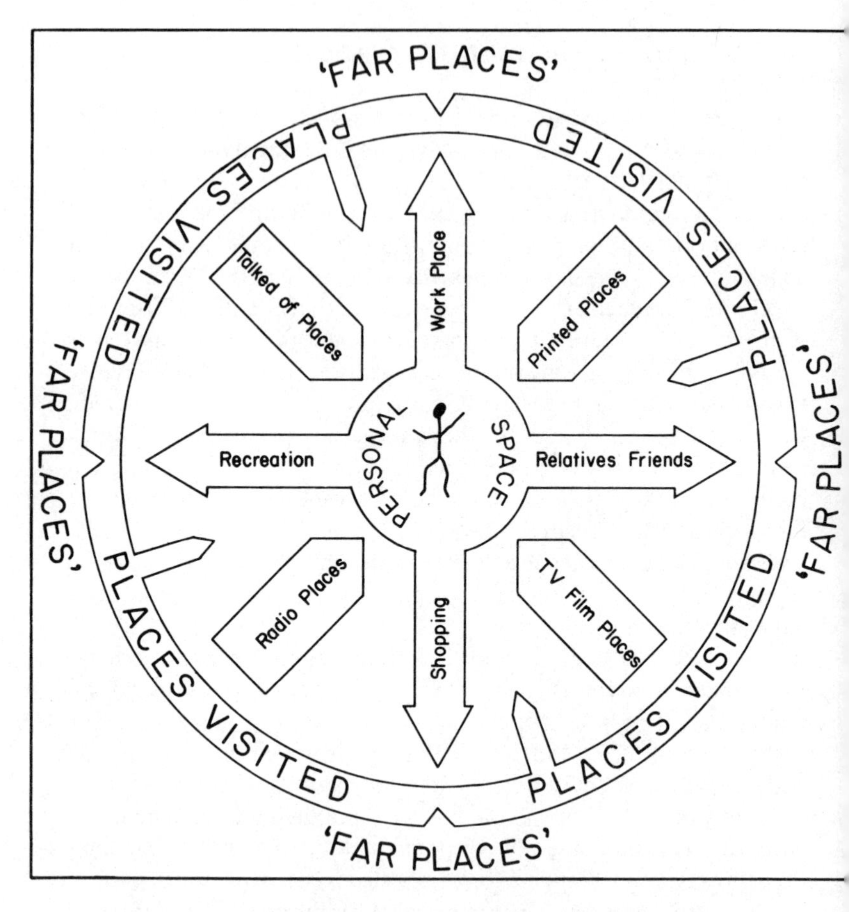

Figure 7.2 Sources of information, types of behaviour and environmental images (Source: Goodey, 1971, p. 7)

destination areas. As there are, for many people, various trip origins as well as trip destinations, the pattern of acquiring knowledge through trip-making behaviour is discontinuous and uneven. However, certain locations tend to act as regular trip origins in everyday life. Such examples are the work-place, school and home, the last being of especial importance in relation to the behaviour of young children (Andrews, 1973). The constraining impact on behaviour and knowledge acquired through the necessity to be at a certain place at a certain time suggests that fruitful links could be forged between studies of image development and time–space budget analyses (Anderson, 1971).

Directional biases are also present in patterns of trip-making behaviour, both reflecting and reinforcing biases in knowledge of the environment. A directional bias in the pattern of residential change in mid-Western cities of the United States has been related to the hypothesised sector-shaped mental maps of the migrants (Adams, 1969). Confirmatory results of a sectorally-biased search area for suburban dwellers were reported for the extensively researched town of Cedar Rapids (Horton and Reynolds, 1971).

It seems that mode of travel is an important determinant of the amount and nature of information yielded by the various trips which people take. Walking yields more detailed information than movement by vehicle, though for a smaller area in a given period of time. It is possible that the onset of mass car ownership, with children chauffered from place to place, has had a marked impact on their comprehension and image of the environment (Schaeffer and Sclar, 1975). Maurer and Baxter (1972), discussing the relationship between children's urban images and mode of travel to school, found that those children travelling by car or bus had a high incidence of structure (shops, factories, houses) and pathway elements in their images, and children travelling by bus reported images similar to those of Lynch's adult subjects. On the other hand, those walking to school made little reference to structures other than houses, but great reference to natural environment elements—trees, grass, sky, sun, animals. These differences were found among a large sample of children aged between 7 and 14 years, including black, white and Mexican American children. Differences in mode of travel to school were suggested as the reason for contrasts in adjustment and performance among primary school children in Devon (Lee, 1957). There was a progressive decline in adjustment with length of journey to school, especially amongst those brought by public or private transport. It was suggested that this reflected the perceived inaccessibility of home by the transported child, who registered a disconnected set of images, with the home schema separated from the school schema by terra incognita, a psychological barrier of many hours' duration breachable only with outside aid.

In general, trip-making behaviour can be divided into two types: spatial search behaviour, involving visiting places for the first time, and habitual spatial behaviour, involving repeated trips to particular locations. Compared to the latter, patterns of spatial search are a relatively neglected area within geography and the social sciences generally (Silk, 1971). This neglect in geography has existed despite the role of spatial search in the build-up of environmental images and the evolution of more stable behaviour patterns, and perhaps reflects the impact of normative location theories such as those of Christaller (1966), Isard (1956) and Losch (1954) which assume total knowledge of all relevant factors and locations. Such work as has been carried out on spatial search has tended to concentrate on normative or conceptual approaches (Golledge, 1967; 1969; Gould, 1966; Silk, 1971). However, a few empirical studies of spatial search strategies have been made in spheres as diverse as consumer behaviour (Hudson, 1975) and industrial location and relocation (Keeble, 1971; Townroe, 1974).

The intensity and spatial extent of search varies with the reasons for search, prior knowledge of where to search (which implies knowledge from secondary sources) and the person or organisation involved in search. These variations have implications for the build-up of environmental images. For example, a person would tend to search more extensively when looking for a new house than for a new grocery store to patronise — but in both cases locations searched would reflect existing information of places likely to meet perceived needs. For example, estate agents' advertisements may lead to searching particular parts of the city when looking for a new house. Similarly, while an expanding multi-national company seeking locations in which to increase its productive capacity will have a spatially more extensive search area than the house-hunter, its search pattern will be equally partial and spatially discontinuous at each of its different levels of operation – initially between possible countries, then between competing regions in the chosen country – before selecting an actual site (Blackbourn, 1973). Again, locations searched would reflect the image of various places in relation to the company's requirements (some aspects of which are discussed in the following chapter).

Thus much spatial search activity represents a behavioural hypothesis-testing process, based on knowledge acquired from secondary sources and in turn yielding additional knowledge as a result of direct, first-hand knowledge of such locations. This is also true of knowledge yielded in connection with patterns of routine behaviour, with the added qualification that previous trips may have been important in shaping the image. That many patterns of behaviour *are* routine and repetitive – journeys to work, or shop, or leisure – both implies a certain stability of environmental image and is the reason that such trips can be successfully described in terms of some variant of the gravity model (see Wilson, 1971). Such trips are made regularly in response to given requirements, in relation to the constraints which may influence behaviour, and knowledge as to where these requirements can be satisfied. Objects and places take on meaning via these interactions. Trips yield knowledge which either confirms or rejects hypotheses – images – of the utility of places in relation to perceived needs, as well as possibly yielding additional information about the environment, such as land-use changes along the journey to work route. Unconfirmed hypotheses may lead to further patterns of spatial search, changed aspirations or revision of environmental images to cope with dissonant findings.

It is clear that the distinction between primary and secondary sources as analytic categories should not disguise the fact that these are complementary in the development of environmental images. But while little attention has been given to primary sources, the role of secondary sources in environmental image development is perhaps both more complex and more neglected (Gold, 1974). The decisive feature of secondary sources – mass-media or interpersonal contact – is that they can convey images both of familiar places and environments and of places and environments with which people have no direct contact, images of what have been termed 'Far Places' (Goodey, 1971: see figure 7.1). But at the same time the mass media convey images filtered through the experience, values and aims of others. Discussion of the role of secondary sources can be structured around three themes: the production and projection of the image; the transmission of the image; the image as received.

While environmental images may be conveyed through the first-hand experience of other people, the main secondary source of information that contributes to the development of environmental images is the mass media – newspapers, journals, books; radio, television, film – although this is not to deny that the image emitted by these sources may be mediated through one or more persons rather than going directly to its final destination. In any case, the image as produced and projected through the mass media necessarily involves the producers' image of what is interesting or important. The numerous producers of these images can be classified into one of two main types: individuals and organisations. As these individuals and organisations have different purposes in producing particular images, understanding of the projected image requires consideration of these purposes. This diversity of purpose makes generalisation rather difficult. The most straightforward path is through a series of short examples, mainly concerned with images projected by various organisations. The reasons for particular individuals projecting particular environmental images in their work are not always clear and this issue is considered in the following chapter in terms of images of north and south in Great Britain.

However, there are also difficulties associated with examining images projected by corporate bodies and organisations. A central problem concerns the identity and aims of the key decision makers in regard to the images created and advanced, partly as a result of problems of access to data. Such research as has been carried out has been mainly concerned with those involved at a tactical level in the lower eschelons of the decision hierarchy, rather than with those at the top, whose strategic decisions are of decisive importance in constraining the limits of the projected image (Gold, 1974). Therefore, while it is reasonable to postulate the existence of a hierarchy of decision makers, 'gatekeepers' whose actions lead to the image produced, with the limits for initiatives narrowed as one descends the hierarchy, neither the precise nature of the relations between levels nor, crucially, the identity and aims of the decisive decision makers is usually clear.

Particularly important in shaping environmental images, especially of 'far places', are the various organisations involved in the daily presentation of news through the different media. As presented, the news reflects both the images and aims of those in power in the producing organisation, and their expression in corporate or editorial policy. This is important in effectively 'defining the agenda' of issues for discussion, acting as a series of filters to exclude or include events as 'news'. Such filters operate at a variety of levels. For example, *Pravda* serves as a national-level filter within the USSR, its content and mode of presentation of the 'truth' being closely controlled by the State. While the news media in the United Kingdom are traditionally conservative in outlook, there is variety in the approach of different newspapers to the 'same' events and spatial biases in the coverage of news – and so of the image projected.

This varying degree of spatial coverage reflects the interaction of four factors. First, there is a negative relationship between the degree of coverage given to places and their distance from the centre and sphere of operations of the producing organisation. In Britain, for example, the *Glasgow Herald,* the *Newcastle Journal* and the *Birmingham Post* devote particular attention to daily occurrences in their respective regions. Similarly, regionally-based television companies and radio stations concentrate on providing information about their home areas via special local news programmes, in addition to coverage of national events. Little wonder, then, that children's and adults' knowledge of place show similar spatial biases (see figure 7.3). In contrast, a newspaper such as *The Times* concentrates on issues of 'national' concern, though internationally a similar distance – decay effect is observable. It has been argued that the emergence of the concept of 'nation' depended on the growth of newspapers as an important communications medium (Rapoport, 1974).

A second factor concerning spatial coverage is reflected in the positive relationship between coverage given and overall importance of a place on the world stage. For example, the British press pays more attention to events in large cities, particularly capital cities such as New York or Geneva influential in world affairs, than to smaller towns, such as Tulare, California. This, together with the 'distance – decay' effect mentioned above, is evident in the spatial distribution of BBC news correspondents on a global scale (see figure 7.4). Gould and White (1974, p. 131) argue that the amount of information about places is a non-linear function of these two variables alone, being positively related to population and negatively related to distance.

Third, more attention is given by the news media to cities that have particular historical or contemporary significance for a country's inhabitants. For example, British entry to the EEC made Brussels a place of greater significance, while events in the capital cities of the countries of the Commonwealth are of more interest to the British public than, say, the French. However, such uneven spatial coverage can also operate in a counter-intuitive direction. One might expect the French people to be most interested in the countries and cultures of their European neighbours and this to be reflected in the output of the French media. Yet minimal coverage is given to these issues on French TV and European unity is a topic virtually banished from discussion. The reason for this selective filtering of spatial information is the policy of the French government, again pointing to the

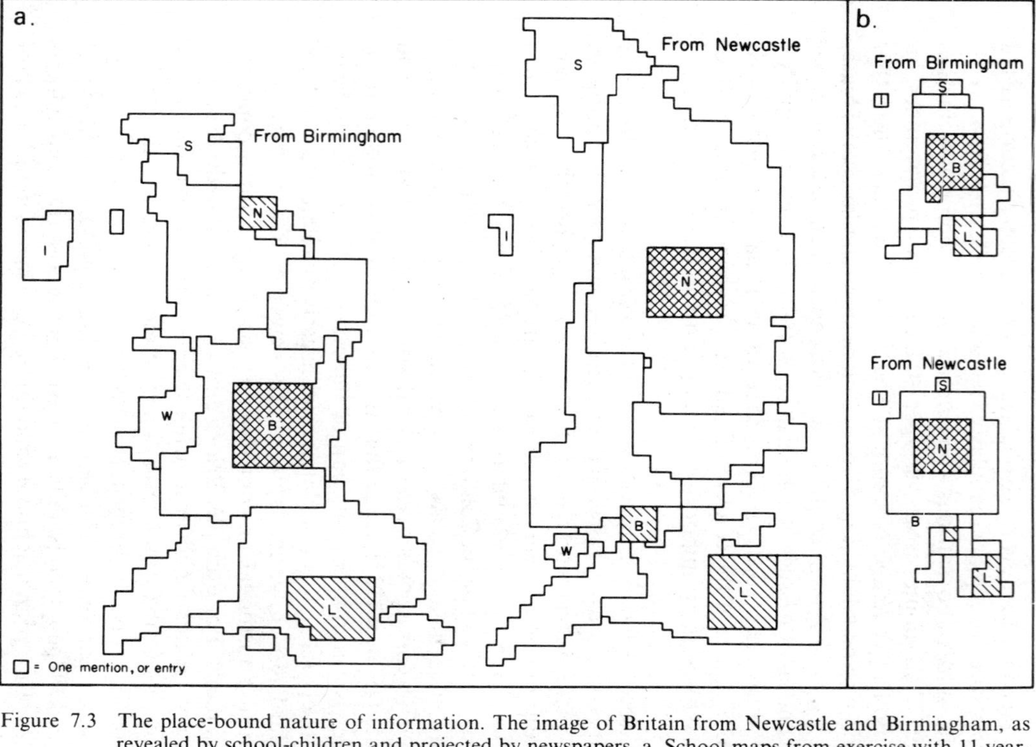

Figure 7.3 The place-bound nature of information. The image of Britain from Newcastle and Birmingham, as revealed by school-children and projected by newspapers. a, School maps from exercise with 11 year-olds requesting first 25 places that they could think of (Brandwood, 1968); b, Newspaper maps from content analysis of two morning newspapers, *The Journal* and *The Birmingham Post* (both for 27 April 1976). Boundaries are those of Economic Planning Regions. Abbreviations: B, Birmingham; I, Ireland;

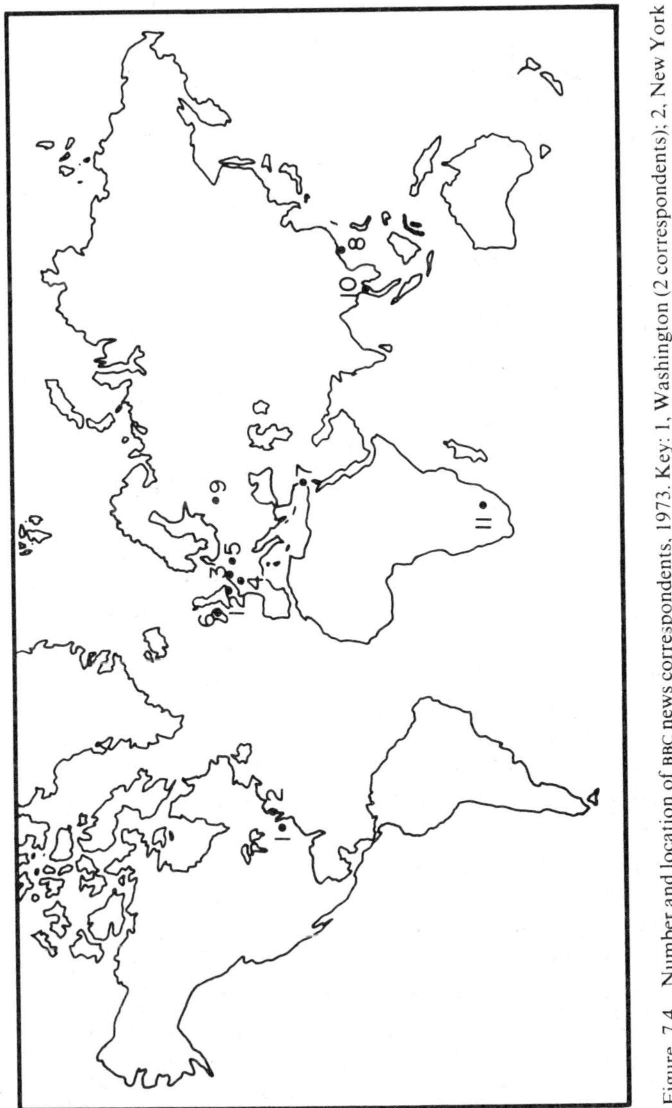

Figure 7.4 Number and location of BBC news correspondents, 1973. Key: 1, Washington (2 correspondents); 2, New York (2); 3, Brussels (1); 4, Paris (1); 5, Wiesbaden (1); 6, Dublin (1); 7, Beirut (2); 8, Hong Kong (1); 9, Moscow (1); 10, Bangkok (1); 11, Johannesburg (1); 12, London (12) (Source: Goodey, 1974*a*, p. 84)

close relationship between State policies and images as projected through the media. A final point is that places, which for some reason are of current news value, tend to be given prominence by the media in the short term: for example, a bank robbery in a normally quiet suburban high street or a revolution in a Third World state, can thrust an unsuspecting place temporarily into the spotlight.

Presentation of 'news' and the projected environmental images that this implies results, broadly, from a combination of commercial and educational (in the broadest sense of the term) aims. Such aims are now discussed further in terms of the images of the place projected by advertising organisations and by the educational system. Advertising is the world of persuasion, whether by 'hidden' means through appealing to our subconscious thought processes (Packard, 1957) or by visual or aural means (Thomas, 1967), aimed at selling a commodity, service or place by projecting an irresistibly attractive image. Thus, in the present context the estate agent offers his 'desirable residence', the commercial developer his 'prestigious site', the industrial promotions officer his district at the 'hub of communications' – a theme taken up in the following chapter.

Gould and White (1974) suggest that differences in the perceived desirability of the contiguous states of Kentucky and West Virginia in the United States, as seen by a group of California university students, reflects the impact of advertising. Both are areas of considerable social and economic distress but Kentucky, projected in many advertisements as a land of blue grass pastures and white fences, is evaluated much more favourably than is West Virginia.

A particularly interesting example of the links between advertising and images of place is provided by travel and tourist agencies, where there may be marked contrasts between the glamorous world projected by the glossy brochure which the tourist can – and usually does – experience and the more mundane, perhaps poverty-ridden world of the indigenous inhabitants. The aim of the brochure is less to accurately inform than to sell the product – the holiday – and place.

In contrast to advertising, the aim of the education system is usually held to be to accurately inform. From primary to tertiary levels, the education system clearly plays an important role in the formation and transmission of images of places and environments. Unlike Hardy's Tess, we are no longer dependent on the teaching of the local school for a judgement of places beyond the confines of the immediate locality. Nevertheless, formal education fulfils a vital role in the acquisition of knowledge and evaluations of both 'near' and 'far' places during the child's formative years. However, it is vital not to overstress the importance of formal education in some parts of the contemporary world. A study of US schoolchildren's images of Africa, for instance, revealed that despite the fact that the children had recently studied Africa at school, their images of the area were shaped more by popular culture than by the formal educational system (Hicks and Beyer, 1968).

The particular images projected by the education system reflect an interplay between the value systems of teachers, syllabuses and textbooks. It is salutary to balance the seemingly authoritative word of the printed text with Curry's reminder that such works are 'perceptions passed through the double filter of the author's mind and his available tools for argument and representation' (Curry, 1962, p. 21).

Even without overt state-imposed ideological strictures, the end product of the formal education system in Britain has traditionally been nationalistic, or at best Eurocentric, in outlook (Cole, 1959). Depiction of the British Empire on map projections maximising the pink land areas is an obvious example of the stuff from which such an end product emerged. Moreover, it is a universal feature for the geographical content of standard schoolbooks to give children more information about their home area and its peoples than of other places and their people (Gould and White, 1974, p. 146). During this century the State has come to play an increasing role in specifying syllabuses, which places shall form the elements of a geography syllabus as well as what information shall be conveyed about these by, for example, specifying course texts. The question of the role of the State and why the State should wish to project certain environmental images is taken up in succeeding chapters.

Discussion of the education system inevitably involves touching on the transmission as well as production of images. While images can be transmitted direct by the various media, it is perhaps more common for them to be mediated through a third party. This has been recognised in the various suggested models of communication through the media (figure 7.5). The single-step or 'hypodermic needle' model, so called because of a hypothesised mechanical response, shares much in common with stimulus – response conceptualisations of behaviour, postulating a direct flow of information from communicator to audience who then adopt the (desired)

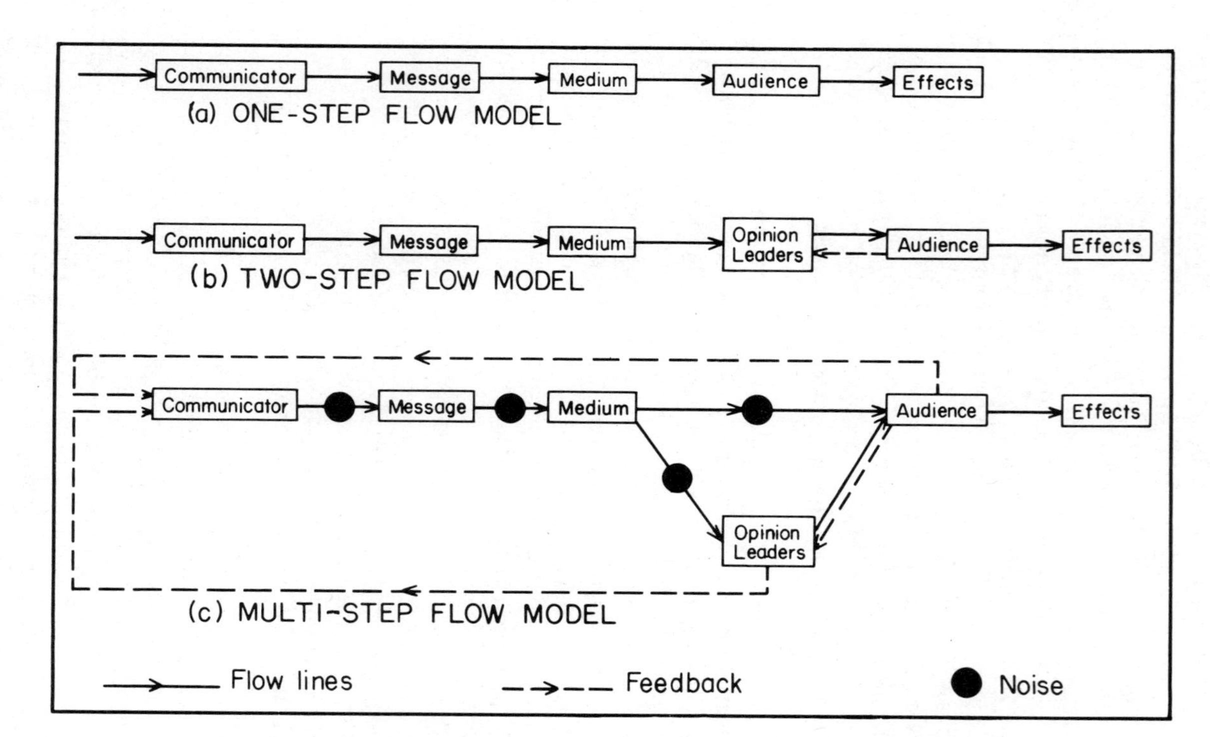

Figure 7.5 Three models of mass media communication (Source: Gold, 1974, p. 10)

communicator's viewpoint. The two-stage model views information as flowing from the media to influential individuals, 'opinion leaders', who act as gatekeepers to selectively pass on this information to the rest of the population. However, such a two-step model does not allow that people be directly influenced by the media nor that people at times take on the role of 'leader', at other times that of 'follower'. The recognition of these limitations led to the emergence of the multi-step model, allowing information to reach individuals both directly and indirectly through a variety of channels and for the existence of 'noise' feedback loops, combining aspects of the earlier 'hypodermic needle' and two-stage models and extending them (Gold, 1974).

The emphasis on interpersonal contact in conveying images and information in the two-step and multi-step models of communication provides links with other areas of concern in geography. Interpersonal contact has assumed importance in relation to studies of contact fields (Goddard, 1971*a*) and in conceptualising the process of diffusion of artifacts over space, where it has been posited to be the primary transmitting mechanism (Brown and Moore, 1969; Hagerstrand, 1968). Patterns of interpersonal contact can be thought of as structured via a variety of social relationships. The family is clearly an important source of knowledge and opinion. Various role relationships in organisations or groups constrain interpersonal contacts and the range of events and interpretations of events to which individuals are exposed. More generally, class structures and relationships control access to amounts and types of knowledge and so help produce and reproduce various composite environmental images — as is tacitly recognised in the two-step and multi-step models of communication.

The last point for discussion, having considered images as produced and projected through the media and the transmission of these images, is their end product — the image as received. While the precise impacts depend on the medium, the message and the receiver, in general terms those of the media are marked, both on images of places directly known and those not visited.

The printed word of the novel may conjure up vivid place, or regional, consciousness (see chapter 8). Its influence is no less strong whether or not the particular environment is known at first hand, while anyone coming to an area previously known only through the field of literature may well find the experience confirmatory – the newcomer is already prepared to 'see what he knows'. Examples of the influence of literature abound. The American visitor's preconception of London towards the end of the last century, for instance, was 'pre-eminently Dicken(s)y' (Weatherbee, 1886, p. 937). Doubtless, because of ideological filters, the same view may still be held by East Europeans today. The particular bias projected by the British Travel Association of royal pageantry amid historic and literary-rich London is hardly a modern image. Beyond London, the official Tourist Board literature introduces what it calls the 'eleven faces of England' which stretch 'From King Arthur's domain in the west to the wild frontier kingdom of Northumbria. From Constable Country to Wordsworth Country. From the White Cliffs of Dover to the Hunting Shires' (English Tourist Board, 1974, pp. 4–5). Little wonder, that results of descriptor-type exercises in America to elicit the image of Britain should emphasise London, the monarchy, history, rustic landscape, etc. (Cole, 1972; Goodey, 1974*c*). Or that ethno-centric perception in general should consist to a large extent of time-bound stereotypes or caricatures, for example between Britain and America (Cooke, 1975; Honour, 1976) or between the British and the French (Faber, 1976).

Although the printed word retains certain advantages, and traditionally has been supreme, the influence of television today is far-reaching and its potential for image creation great. The popular image of the contemporary American city, it is suggested (Berry, 1970), largely reflects the image as projected through the medium of television, while the white flight to the suburbs is another reflection of this stereotype. At another level of spatial resolution, a study of American school children's images of Africa south of the Sahara, revealed that from a group of 90 stimulus words, the third most frequently chosen after 'wild animals' and 'elephants' was *Daktari*, a popular television programme (Hicks and Beyer, 1968).

The perceived power of this relatively new medium is highlighted by the concern of local or regional officials when a 'wrong', and therefore harmful, image is portrayed on the screen. For example, witness the call of Kirkby councillors and community leaders for the BBC to stop using their town as the locale for the crime series *Z Cars* (*The Times*, 23 October 1974). Or again, the meetings between the N.W. Industrial Development Association with both the BBC and Independent Television over their portrayals of a 'rather adverse image' which they considered was hindering the Association's efforts to attract new industry (*The Times*, 26 January 1973).

CONCLUSION

In this chapter, a number of issues concerning information sources and the development of environmental images have been discussed. Generalising about the variety of sources of information that contribute to the development of environmental images, it is clear that primary sources, involving direct contact with the environment, are of critical importance in youth. But while this remains an important source for many purposes, as people age secondary sources take on an increasingly important role. This is especially true with regard to images of 'far places'. Images acquired from secondary sources often prove very durable and resistant, particularly when such images are acquired in childhood. This emphasises the critical role of the education system in shaping images of environments and space.

Issues concerning differential access to specific types of information about places are considered in a planning context in the next two chapters. A major issue in planning is the different images of the 'same' environment held by different people, the reasons for these differences and the seeds of conflict, actual or potential, that these can sow. Much planning activity is devoted to reducing or eliminating discrepancies in images, either by material resource allocations or by issuing particular streams of information designed to produce desired changes in images. This latter issue is taken up again in the following chapter.

8 Environmental Images, and Planning and Policy Implications I

As a prelude to a more general discussion of the role and utility of environmental images in relation to planning, and in order to develop certain themes raised in the previous chapter, attention is here focused on the importance of secondary sources in image formation, with an illustration of their influence at the regional level of resolution. The justification for this emphasis is that, despite modern mobility, man is still dependent to a considerable extent on secondary sources for his information of 'far places'. The cumulative influence of schooling and vicarious experiences through the arts and popular mass media enable him to know, and hold opinions about, many places never actually visited. The general type of mental representation so formed may be considered an imagination-image, being simpler, less rounded and containing a higher degree of distortion than is found in a memory-image (Tuan, 1975, p. 211). The relative proportions of these qualities can be the basis for a more precise subdivision – stereotype, an *over*simplification; myth, an ill-founded over-simplification; prejudice, an oversimplification unresponsive to corrective, first-hand evidence (Allport, 1954). Examples of these will be evident in the following descriptions, although the generic term image is generally preferred.

Secondary sources, then, enable a filling-in of *terra incognita*. They are also important in influencing, by implanted expectations or conditioning, image formation of those areas subsequently known at first hand. Therefore, an obvious contrast exists between the image of a place held by the resident native and that held by the outsider. This is seen in the replies to two sample population studies in the city of Hull (Burgess, 1974). Both groups made a few common selections from an adjectival checklist of 48 items such as 'docks', 'ships' and 'fishy', but only the city's inhabitants emphasised elements of general structure, such as 'shopping facilities' and 'redevelopment', or positive affection, for example 'friendly' and 'parks'. Outsiders emphasised the negative attributes – 'heavy industry', 'unemployment', 'slums', 'smoke', etc. (see table 8.1). The non-native sample was in fact presenting the stereotype of a nineteenth-century industrial town in the north of England, illustrating the general property of stereotyped images, namely the subsuming of individual variety within a broad generic type. Thus through its oversimplification, the stereotype becomes applicable to many cases or to a wide area.

TABLE 8.1

LEADING CHARACTERISTIC ATTRIBUTES OF HULL AS PERCEIVED BY INHABITANTS AND OUTSIDERS

Inhabitants	%	*Outsiders*	%
Good shopping centre	85	Docks	90
Working-class city	84	Working-class city	85
Docks	81	Ships	79
Large council estates	75	Fishy	75
Friendly	74	Heavy industry	67
Trees, parks	74	Slums	63
Ships	65	Large council estates	59
Low wages	61	Unemployment	57
Fishy	58	Cold	56
Congested traffic	57	Smoke	53
Tower block flats	56	Congested traffic	50
Redevelopment	55	Drabness	49

Responses in percentages. $N = 180$ for both groups.

Source: Burgess (1974), p. 169.

The origin and propagation of imagination-images is determined by the communication process through which, in the absence of first-hand information, a few common sources achieve widespread acceptance. This is illustrated at regional level, where established intellectual and literary channels for the past hundred and fifty years have projected a consistent image of 'the north' in sharp contrast, overt or implied, to that of the south, so that the country has come to be seen in this way. The contribution of this dichotomous image to the so-called 'drift to the south', although not quantifiable, must be substantial. Its potential may be gauged from the recent efforts among planners at all levels to project a counter-image to attempt to stem out-migration from peripheral regions.

THE IMAGE OF NORTH AND SOUTH AS PROJECTED

The theme of north and south, intertwined with the associated ones of London and the provinces or city versus country (Knoepflmacher, 1973; Williams, 1973), came strongly into focus during the nineteenth century as industrialisation both helped reinforce the existing contrasts and created new ones. Not only 'regional' novelists (Bentley, 1941; Gilbert, 1960), but poets, travellers and commentators all projected aspects of the same consistent image.

The early Victorian period saw the rise of the social novelist who portrayed aspects of division, primarily in a social dimension but with strong territorial correlates. Thus, Disraeli's *Sybil*, written in 1845 and subtitled 'The Two Nations', contrasted the life of the rich in London with that of the poor in the mines of Mowbray (Lancs) and in the metal-working district of Wodgate (near Birmingham). In Mrs Gaskell's *Mary Barton* (1848), subtitled 'A Tale of Manchester Life', the world of the cellar dwellers is the backcloth. Manchester also figures prominently in Mrs Gaskell's later novel, actually called *North and South* (1855). The regional contrast is strongly drawn.

The idyllic life of the heroine, Margaret Hale, in a Hampshire village 'sleeping in the warm light of the pure sun' is abruptly ended when her father resigns from the church and transports his family to Milton (Manchester) in the county of Darkshire to become private tutor to a mill owner. Her initial reaction to the impending move and the perceived difference between the two worlds are illuminating. She wonders 'what in the world do manufacturers want with the classics, or literature, or the accomplishments of a gentleman', for she had in fact

> almost a detestation for all she had ever heard of the North of England, the manufacturers, the people, the wild and bleak country.
>
> (Mrs Gaskell, *North and South*, 1855, chapter 4).

The heroine's worst fears are realised on the approach to their new home:

> For several miles before they reached Milton, they saw a deep lead-coloured cloud hanging over the horizon . . . Nearer the town the air had a faint taste and smell of smoke. Quick they were whirled over long, straight, hopeless streets of regularly-built houses, all small and of brick. Here and there a great oblong many-windowed factory stood up, like a hen among her chickens, puffing out black 'unparliamentary' smoke and sufficiently accounting for the cloud which Margaret had taken to be rain.
>
> (Mrs Gaskell, *North and South*, 1855, chapter 7).

A similar description of a northern mill town is conveyed in Dickens' better known *Hard Times* (1854) where Coketown (Preston) has become *the* epitome or stereotype of the nineteenth century manufacturing town:

> It was a town of red brick, or of brick that would have been red if the smoke and ashes had allowed it; but as matters stood it was a town of unnatural red and black like the painted face of a savage. It was a town of machinery and tall chimneys, out of which interminable serpents of smoke trailed themselves for ever and ever, and never got uncoiled. It had a black canal in it, and a river that ran purple with ill-smelling dye, and vast piles of buildings full of windows where there was a rattling and trembling all day long . . . You saw nothing in Coketown but what was severely workful . . . The jail might have been the infirmary, the infirmary might have been the jail, the town-hall might have been either, or both, or anything else . . .
>
> (Dickens, *Hard Times*, 1854, chapter 5).

The contrast between the world of industrialisation compared with the peaceful world of Eliot's Loamshire, Trollope's Barsetshire, 'Jefferies' Land, in Wiltshire, or Hardy's Wessex could hardly be more complete. Although life in rural Wessex, for instance, may not have been easy for all, it probably was for the bulk of the novelist's readers, who needed little willing suspension of disbelief to perceive an unspoilt landscape. Man's greatest intrusion, for instance, the town of Casterbridge (Dorchester), could be described as:

> untouched by the faintest sprinkling of modernism . . . compact as a box of dominoes . . . behind a dense stockade of limes and chestnuts, set in the midst of miles of rotund down and concave field
>
> (Hardy, *The Mayor of Casterbridge*, 1886, chapter 4).

In contrast, the reading public might well reflect on the fact that the outstanding depiction of a non-industrial northern landscape by a major novelist of the last century was that of the West Riding moorland in *Wuthering Heights* (Emily Bronte, 1847), a wild and primitive country.

As the century drew to a close the publication of an increasing number of reports on the urban condition (Briggs, 1963; Wohl, 1973) together with the cumulative affect of anti-urbanism among pamphleteers and reformers (Levine, 1973) reinforced the contrast between the north and south. Although the East End of London had become the largest example of urban poverty, the very diversity and counter-attractions of the capital in no way diminished the 'traditional' regional contrast.

After the turn of the century the two major novelists to whom place was important portrayed northern industrial scenes. The 'five towns' of the Potteries were described by Arnold Bennett in the first of his works set in the district as 'long given up to unredeemed ugliness . . . sombre, hardfeatured, uncouth' lying in a 'smoke-girt amphitheatre' (1902, chapter 1). The mining landscapes on the Nottinghamshire – Derbyshire border figure in many of D.H. Lawrence's major novels. The author's lack of sympathy with the type of urban growth spawned by industrialisation – 'red brick rapidly spreading, like a skin disease' (1915, p. 345) – is no less evident in his letters and essays (for example 1929).

Modern, working-class novels set in the industrial Midlands, West Riding or Lancashire by Sillitoe, Storey or Braine, respectively, have done little to disperse the traditional image. In fact, the environmental contrast with the south, implicit or explicit, is still clearly alive in the world of the novel. Braine's (1976) most recent work, for instance, begins amid scenes of northern ugliness, with a stereotyped depiction identical to that found in his first novel (1957); the hero then breaks with his Wigan – Manchester background and flees south to the affluence of a Surrey commuter town, to the comforts that the rising-executive belt of Sugar Hill bring.

The fullest treatment of the north – south theme is found in Orwell's *The Road to Wigan Pier* (1937) where, after recording the pitiful condition of various northern towns now blackened by a century's smoke, the author explores the whole question. Orwell drew a line a little north of Birmingham to demarcate the beginning of the 'real ugliness of industrialisation', an environment to which northerners were conditioned and, therefore, no longer aware. As a southerner venturing north, he was:

> conscious, quite apart from the unfamiliar scenery, of entering a strange country. This is partly because of certain real differences which do exist, but still more because of the north – south antithesis which has been rubbed into us for such a long time past.
> (Orwell, *The Road to Wigan Pier*, 1937, chapter 7).

A 'cult of Northernness', a kind of snobbishness by which the northerner regards anyone to the south of him as inferior, has helped to engender this antithesis. The northerner is thus warm-hearted and hard-working; in contrast the southerner is seen as snobbish, soft and lazy. (Of course an inversion of these same attributes by the southerner sees himself as civilised and living by intelligence rather than brawn, in contrast to the nosey, dogged, aggressive northerners.) The north's image of itself was as a place where wealth was created, and the south as a place where it was squandered – a view that, objectively, is not without substance. This view, quoted by Orwell, is found frequently in northern literature from the middle of the last century, when Brighton was usually chosen as the epitome of southern dissipation. 'All is loss at Brighton', for instance, wrote Praed in 1863, compared with Middlesbrough which was 'an addition to the riches of the world' (Praed, 1863, p. 4).

The theme of wealth creation was taken up at the end of another influential piece of literature in the interwar period, J.B. Priestley's *English Journey* (1934). Here it is a northerner reporting and, as such, he assures the reader that his evaluation is 'a reasonable one'. Certainly no sentimentalism or ambivalent attitude to beauty intrudes during his tour of the various depressed industrial regions, whether in the metallic squalor of the Black Country, in the 'hideous' Lancashire mill towns or the 'very scrag ends of industrial life' on Tyneside with Newcastle 'even blacker than Manchester'. What he does frequently do is to contrast the observed conditions with those in the south, and to write passionately about the apparent indifference of southern-based decision makers or news disseminators to that part of the country on which Britain's wealth had been built. At the very end of his travels he summarises the faces of England of the 1930s:

> I had seen England. I had seen lots of Englands. How many? At once, three disengaged themselves from the shifting mass. There was, first, old England, the country of the cathedrals and minsters

and manor houses and inns, of Parson and Squire; guide book and quaint highways and byways England . . . Then, I decided, there is the nineteenth century England, the industrial England of coal, iron, steel, cotton, wool, railways; of thousands of rows of little houses all alike, sham Gothic churches, square-faced chapels, Town Halls, Mechanics' Institutes, mills, foundries, warehouses, refined watering places. Pier Pavilions, Family and Commercial Hotels, Literary and Philosophical Societies, back-to-back houses, detached villas with monkey-trees, Grill Rooms, railway stations, slag heaps and 'tips', dock roads, Refreshment Rooms, doss-houses, Unionist or Liberal Clubs, cindery waste ground, mill chimneys, slums, fried-fish shops, public houses with red blinds, bethels in corrugated iron, good-class drapers' and confectioners' shops, a cynically devastated countryside, sooty and dismal little towns, and still sootier grim fortress-like cities. This England makes up the larger part of the Midlands and the North and exists everywhere . . . this period of England's industrial supremacy began to look like a gigantic dirty trick. . . .

The third England, I concluded, was the new postwar England, belonging far more to the age itself than to this particular island . . . This is the England of arterial and by-pass roads, of filling stations and factories that look like exhibition buildings, of giant cinemas and dance-halls and cafes, bungalows with tiny garages, cocktail bars, Woolworths, motor coaches, wireless, hiking, factory girls looking like actresses, greyhound racing and dirt tracks, swimming pools, and everything given away for cigarette coupons . . .

(Priestley, *English Journey*, 1934, pp. 397–401).

Lesser publications merely reinforced the contrast in less eloquent terms. For the popular reader, for instance, Morton's *In Search of England* (1927) naturally spends little time in 'Industrial England' compared with 'beautiful Old England'; the transition at the Cheshire – Lancashire border is described in terms curiously reminiscent of Mrs. Gaskell. For the more socially motivated, *Britain and the Beast* (1938), with its chapter on the North – East headed 'hills and hells' (Sharp, pp. 141–59), or *The Town that was Murdered* (Wilkinson, 1939) were instances of crossing t's and dotting i's of a pattern by now well established.

Compared with novelists and commentators, the poet's contribution to this pattern has been a lesser, but not insignificant, one. The north, or rather, industry and industrial towns, have been consistently ignored as a topic for verse (Strange, 1968; 1973). On the other hand, poems about the south itself or on national themes for which the south is the evident locale, were not only composed but many were committed to memory by generations of schoolchildren. Such were Kipling's poems on Sussex and the downs, or 'The South Country' of Belloc, to whom the Midlands were 'sodden and unkind'. ('The North Country' in a poem by D.H. Lawrence had air 'dark with north and with sulphur'.) In Browning's 'Home Thoughts from Abroad' the April chaffinch singing on the orchard bow clearly does not relate to a northern county, any more than do Rupert Brooke's English scenes of 'Grantchester'.

The south, then, has been extolled at the expense of the north in poetry no less than in novels or writing in general. Writers may have considered the north simply offered a harsher environment (Sillitoe, 1975, p. 117). Industrialisation, which was initially shunned as a suitable literary topic by a pre-urban and pre-capitalist system of values (Dyos and Wolff, 1973, p. 903), certainly presented an ambivalent or inverted kind of beauty. (It is interesting to note that even L.S. Lowry took several years to overcome the shock of moving to Salford amidst the kind of industrial townscape which became typical of his paintings, whose recent popularity has contributed to the persistence of the stereotype image of the north.) Not least of the reasons is that a disproportionate number of authors have been of southern origin. An early interpretation of this phenomenon was made by Conan Doyle (1888), who saw it as but part of a disproportionate share of general intellectual ability, with London and the south having *per capita* figures over twice those of the Midlands and north.

THE IMAGE AS RECEIVED

The north – south contrast, then, has been presented unequivocally by the written word. The justification for concentrating on secondary sources for this theme is that they represent the articulated and accepted system of values of society – articulated on the whole by the privileged, maybe, but received by another privileged group, who have included political, social and economic decision-makers besides being disseminated more widely through the channels of formal education. Moreover, although it may be argued that today the mass

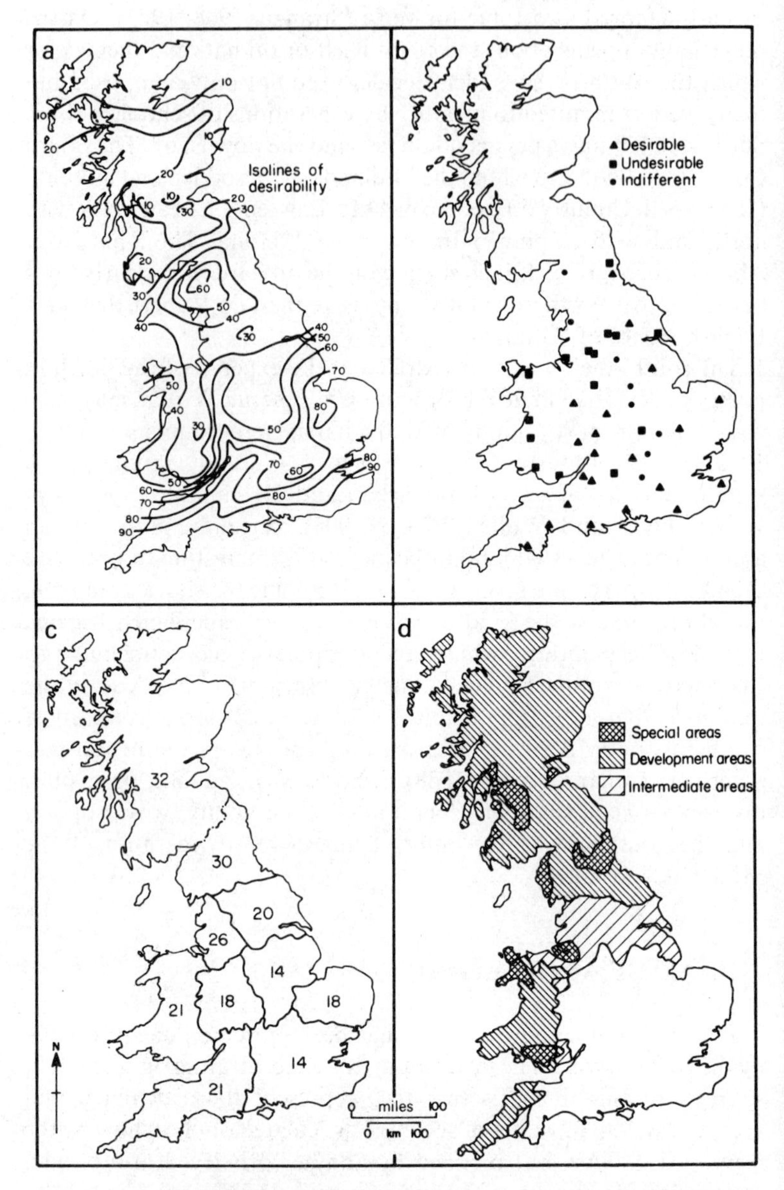

Figure 8.1 Evaluation of different parts of Britain: a, Residential desirability among school-leavers (Gould and White, 1968, p. 172); b, Residential desirability among teachers (Goddard, 1971*b*, unpublished); c, General unattractiveness among businessmen (Business Decision Ltd., 1974, p. 6); d, Special, Development and Intermediate areas

media, especially television, are far more influential, the resilience of the traditionally drawn contrast should not be underestimated. Considering the persistence of the labels of prairie-planning in new towns and middle-class uniformity in the suburbs, despite evidence to the contrary (Thorns, 1972), there is no reason to suppose that the traditional image of the north will rapidly change, be that image technically a stereotype, myth or prejudice. The important landscape is the one in the mind, the imagined one, and consequently in any contest between reality and fiction, the latter is likely to win (Prince, 1973, p. 17). Besides, for those who subscribe to the view that 'seeing is believing', the stereotype image of the north is still very much alive on television screens through working-class plays, serials and period revivals.

The impact of secondary sources, allied to first-hand knowledge, may be seen in maps evaluating or ranking different parts of Britain (figure 8.1). Rankings by school-leavers show the collective or national viewpoint from twenty-three widely dispersed schools (Gould and White, 1968; 1974). Individually, each school produced a dome of high desirability centred on its local area, exhibiting the expected attachment to home territory, together with an assessment of 'far places', based largely on secondary sources, not least of which must have been teachers and textbooks. The isolines of desirability, derived from a list of counties ranked in order of preference as a place to live, highlight the whole of the south coast and diminish to the north. Prongs of desirability extend to Lincolnshire and along counties bordering Wales, leaving Wales itself and the Midlands as troughs. In the north a dome of desirability rises over the Lake District, another lesser one over Edinburgh.

The assessment of cities from the teachers' view of residential desirability presents a similar pattern (figure 8.1b). All cities in the undesirable category are overtly industrial or peripheral, with the exceptions of Swindon and Northampton. Bath, Bristol, Oxford and Cambridge were the most highly desired; at the opposite end of the spectrum were Hull, Bradford, Stoke and Salford.

The regional assessment of attractiveness to businessmen for purposes of industrial relocation, again, presents a similar national distribution of the preference surface (figure 8.1c). The percentage of decision makers believing a region to be undesirable increases with distance from the favoured London and South – East and, in this case, also the East Midland region.

These three maps of spatial preference conform to the traditional pattern which has underlain the so-called 'drift to the south' of population and economic activity since the first world war away from those parts now designated as intermediate, development or special development areas, suggesting that the latent migration potential remains unchanged. This applies to a wide spectrum of activity, and is not simply confined to manufacturing industries or the growth of service industries. Persuasion remains necessary to attract and retain doctors and dentists in the industrial areas such that an inverse care law may be said to exist for medical services (Hart, 1971). Uneven distributions exist for a whole range of social and economic criteria (Coates and Rawstron, 1971). Even ordinands have been described as seeking holy employment rather than holy orders, tending 'to flow to southern areas of relative success as against the conurbations of northern areas of greatest need' (Paul, 1964, p. 147), while 'for writers fresh out of their grim towns . . . such a process – coming "down south" – is like being reborn' (Sillitoe, 1975, p. 108). The last sentiments were sparked by *A Man from the North* (1898), Arnold Bennett's semi-autobiographical novel which opens with a discussion of the 'imperious fascination' of London among certain northerners, as a prelude to the hero leaving Bursley for London and the south. A general awareness of the spatial gradient of the country's social space is evident in its acceptance as a topic for satire (for example Parkinson, 1967).

All of the foregoing, and the fact that a disproportionate amount of perception and decision making is southern or metropolitan-based, is reason enough for the persistence of images based in many instances on a former reality, and indicative of the huge task facing planners and politicians wishing to redress regional imbalance. The frustration that northern planners can feel was illustrated in the amusing mental map issued by the Doncaster and District Development Council (figure 8.2) expressing their idea of how Londoners perceive the country, with civilisation virtually ending at Potters Bar and the railway at Manchester.

To many the north certainly appears as an undifferentiated unit – no more differentiated than the motorway signs to 'The North' which first appear at Watford – such that foreigners may have a clearer picture of its internal variation than visitors from the south (Pocock, 1975, p. 39). A 'legendary North' existed among business managers before their transfer to the Northern Economic Planning

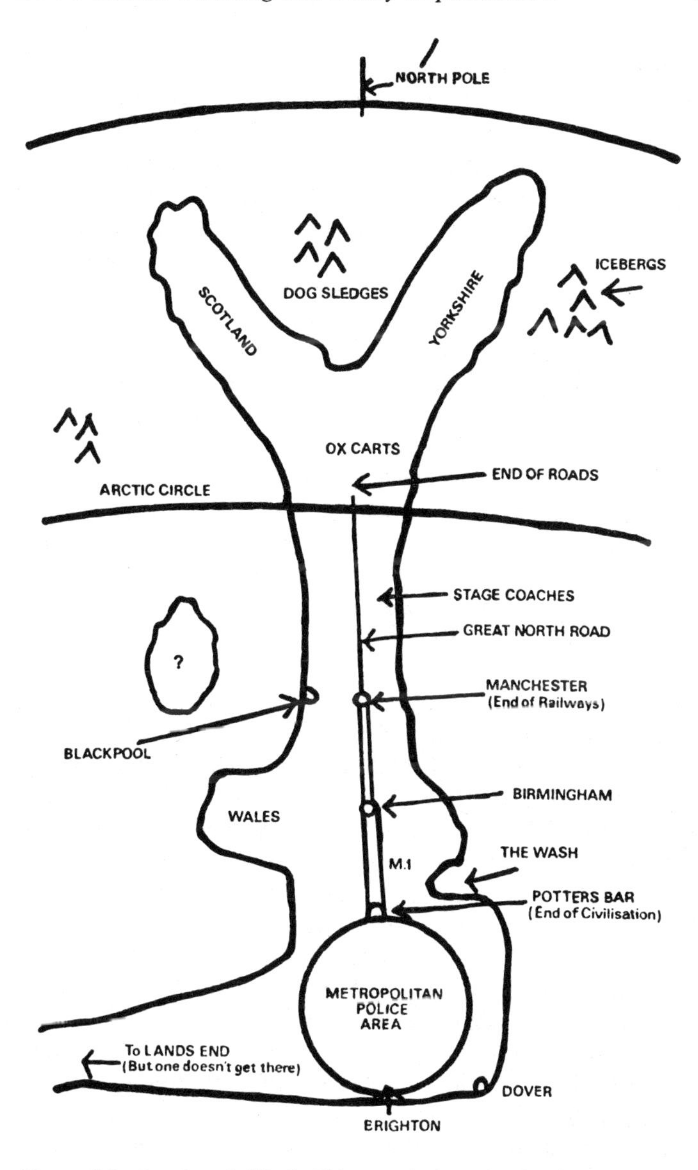

Figure 8.2 'Londoner's View'. This map formed the cover of the 1971 New Year's card sent by Doncaster and District Development Council to leaders of government, politicians, civil servants, and manufacturing companies throughout the Home Counties

Region, which was seen as a land of 'regional isolation, with an unpleasant climate and most of all with an unfavourable urban and industrial landscape' (House *et al.*, 1968, p. 56). Another report on the regional knowledge and attitude of 256 companies that had moved location in Britain revealed a widespread ignorance of locations, characteristics and even names of centres in the north and west (Business Decisions Ltd., 1974). In a mapping exercise, for instance, over one-third failed to place the new towns of Northampton, Corby and Washington within eighty miles of their actual location, the pattern of ignorance increasing northwards. Awareness of promotional advertising by northern centres or areas was generally below one-fifth of the total sample. A massive problem of communication obviously exists, therefore, and a strong counter-image must be projected as a corrective. There are increasing signs that the potential of such a strategy has been realised, in parallel with policies that aim to 'modernise' urban and regional environments by extensive changes to their social, economic and built environments.

THE COUNTER-IMAGE

Although civic pride and economic competitiveness in Britain has hardly given rise to widespread use of city nicknames and booster imagery compared with the United States (Kane and Alexander, 1965; Tuan, 1974*a*, pp. 201–4), an increasing number of authorities now engage in 'P.R.' campaigns, often from their own public or press information department. Their work, particularly active among new towns (Goodey, 1974*c*, pp. 121–33), involves exhibitions – often in London – and various forms of promotional advertising, extending even to postal slogans. The geographical distribution of local authorities using postmarks as a booster image reveals, if not a north – south dichotomy, at least a good surrogate with half of them aiming to attract industrial growth by promoting advantages of land, labour, capital or position, the other half projecting themselves as friendly, sunny holiday centres (figure 8.3). The only locational anomalies are Bradford in the north, which sees itself as the 'base camp for touring Yorkshire' (Leeds having already pre-empted the economic capital tag), and Woking in the south, where the invitation to 'progress' with the town possibly reflects anxieties in its important aviation industry. Only two towns, Hawick and Cardiff, offer

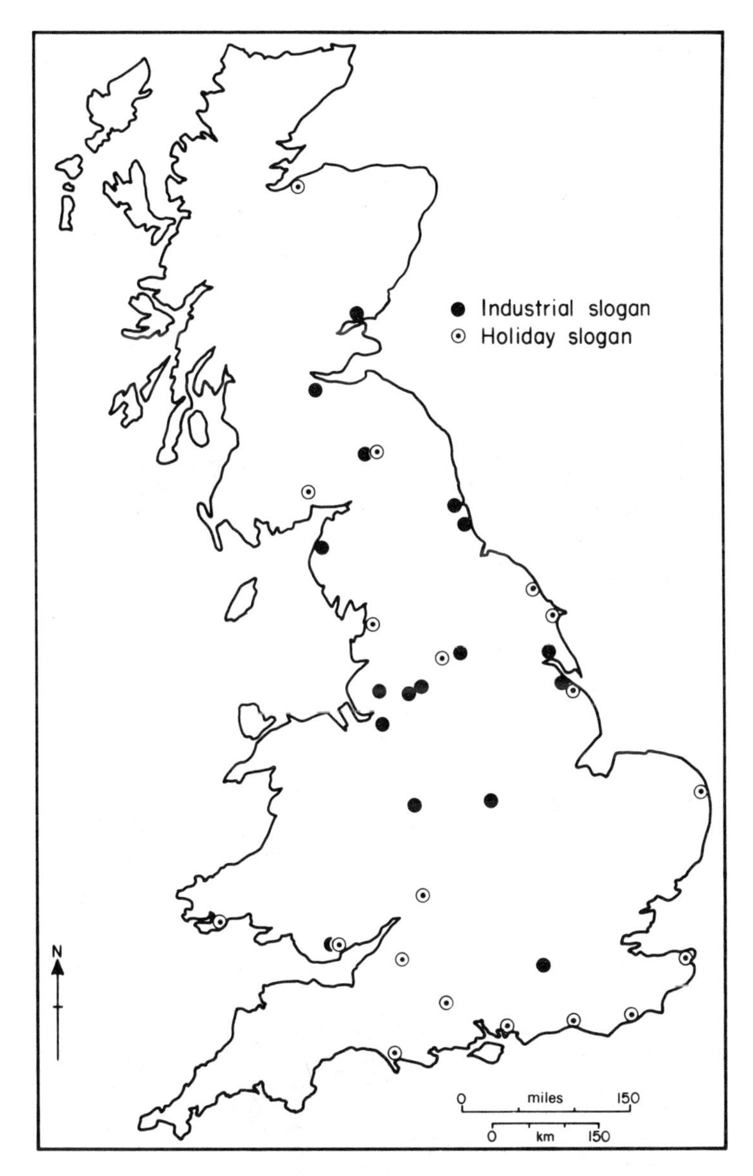

Figure 8.3 Local authorities using postmark slogans, 1975–76, as a booster image. Slogans for anniversaries or special events are omitted. (British Philatelic Bureau)

themselves as centres in which to combine both business and holiday.

A key quality projected is that of accessibility, most easily achieved of course from a central location. Hence the frequent image projection of a centre, heart, hub or capital. The claim to be at the centre ranges from Swindon in the south to Leeds in the north, and from Redditch in the west to Corby in the east (figure 8.4). Moreover, centrality does not inhibit contact with the periphery. Corby, for instance, 'right at the very centre', at the same time has 'good access to major ports'. Even the peripherally located Cwmbran has links 'with every major market in Britain'. Transport, particularly the prestige of the motorway, is the secret. It is a prime psychological boost to be able to offer motorway access, for its presence promises

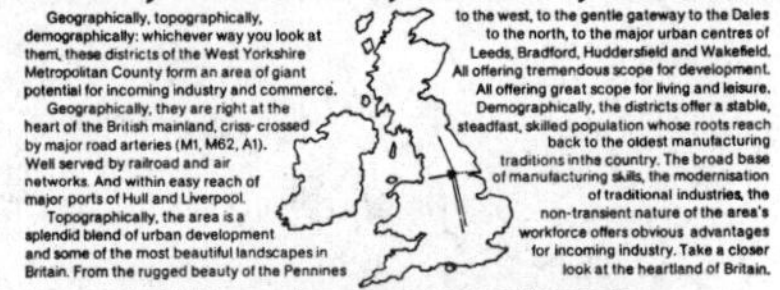

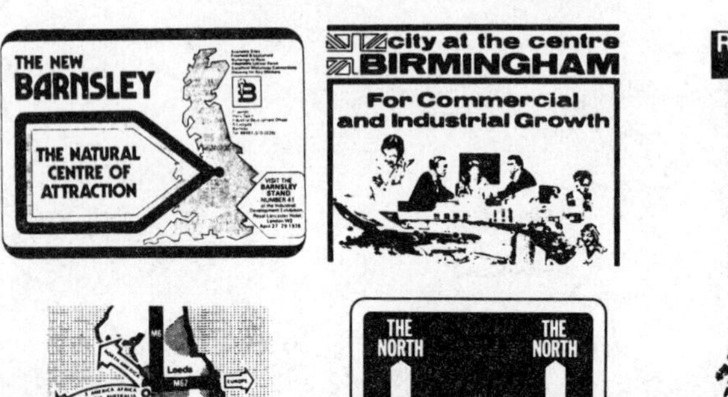

Figure 8.4 Booster imagery and the importance of accessibility

wide linkage. To Rotherham, for instance, the M18 link is 'Euroway'. It is sufficient just to be able to advertise that the motorway 'is coming' (Skelmersdale). What advantage is held, then, by towns that can claim to be a motorway hub (various West Midland authorities) or, simply, 'a motorway city' (Leeds, Rotherham, Glasgow)?

Where a position is unequivocally peripheral, then accessibility can be projected as the 'gateway' or 'spearhead' to an important part of the country or, if on the east coast, to Europe (Hull, Peterlee). The alternative to inverting the perspective or broadening the scale to proclaim an ideal location within a wider context, is to make a bold statement of faith that the town is 'in the right place' (Skelmersdale) or simply 'the place to be' (Peterlee).

In view of the advertised advantages, it is perhaps little wonder that there should be several towns claiming to be the most successful or fastest growing, or that most of the problems encountered by industrialists have been solved. The projected ideal combination of qualities of the environment – natural, built and social – have contributed to this success.

New towns, of course, have led in the promotion of a new environment, bringing 'a new way of life' (Washington) or just 'life back into living' (E. Kilbride), although an image of unrelieved newness could appear deficient in an era increasingly conservation and heritage conscious. In consequence any historical artefact or association is fully exploited; there is now a '250-year-old new town' (Telford), while Northern Ireland has a 'historic new town' (Londonderry). Even to be counted among those designated in the first phase of new town creations is projection-worthy since it emphasises a maturity. Established industrial towns, in contrast, wish to lose the 'old' tag and to be seen pre-eminently as 'new' or as cities 'of the seventies' (for example Manchester, Leeds, Bradford, West Bromwich). The formation of larger authorities in the 1974 local government reorganisation fostered a degree of credence to the new epithets.

Another widespread quality is access to some of the most attractive scenery in Britain (from Wolverhampton, Rotherham, Teesside) or even Europe (Cumbernauld). Access is often undefined, although here modern mobility has undoubtedly added credence to hyperbole, at least for some. Even the climate of the north can be portrayed more attractively than has been traditionally the case. Thus, selection of particular criteria has shown the climate of Fife to be equal to that of South-eastern England (Glenrothes Development Corporation,

1963). Again, by a judicious re-siting of its weather-recording station Bridlington has been able to present 'the true figures'.

The man-made aspects of the climate in northern industrial cities has seen the recent banishment of smoke. Sheffield, for instance, traditionally 'obscured by smoke' and characterised by the smell of sulphur except when that of gas was stronger (Orwell, 1937, p. 95), was by the 1970s projecting itself as possessing 'the cleanest air of any industrial city in Europe'. Again, the smoke which once enveloped Middlesbrough and which was accepted as a necessary concomitant of the Teesside iron and steel industry – although it could be interpreted as a symbol of prosperity and therefore something of which to be proud (Sockett, 1899, p. 44) – has now been banished. The change is epitomised by the document issued by the British Steel Corporation announcing its giant new Redcar steel plant, which, it was claimed (1972, p. 16), would be 'unlikely' to release 'any smoke'. Moreover, air pollution control on existing Teesside works was already so stringent that the fall-out of dust and grit was only one-third that experienced in the City of London (1972, p. 18).

CONCLUSION

It was only during the 1960s that the importance of factors other than those traditionally held important in industrial location decisions began to be widely recognised. Having said that, however, it must be remembered that in an economy dominated by capitalist rationality, in the final analysis, the key consideration in industrial and commercial decision making is the expected rate of return from capital invested, so that strictly economic considerations remain at the heart of such decisions. Thus it is not that these have ceased to be of importance; rather that since the 1960s they have increasingly been expressed in terms of factors other than those held important in 'traditional' industrial location theories.

In an era when variations in transport costs were shown to be small (Chisholm, 1966, pp. 182–8), it became apparent that businessmen were looking not simply for the officially projected 'room to expand' but rather for where the 'grass was greener' (Hall, 1970). An emphasis was therefore turned on the living environment or social infrastructure, including cultural and recreational facilities. Thus the plethora of golf courses has been cited as a critical factor in the inducement of industry to Edinburgh, the historic and scenic variety of Tayside won Dundee its largest manufacturing concern, and first-division soccer is seen as an important asset by the North-east Development Council. (The winning of the FA cup was considered equivalent to a six-figure advertisement for Sunderland and the region (Derrick and McRory, 1973).)

The world of projective or booster images, based on exclusive selection and absolutist viewpoints, is one of alien geographies, although the distortion – like that of the artist – should be for the benefit of truth. Truth in this context is the correcting and replacing of prejudices by some positive qualities of place. In a densely populated and resource-conscious country like Britain, it is imperative to achieve some optimum distribution of work, residence and leisure patterns on both a national and regional scale. At a regional level, in the field of leisure planning, attempts are being made to relieve pressure from the excessive use of a few locations by diversionary signposting and the deliberate stimulation of alternative 'honeypots'. At national level, in the realm of economic planning, Chisholm, in querying whether we must all live in the South-east, wonders

> what would happen if the women's magazines began persistently to extol the virtues of having a house with a garden *and* a husband who came home to lunch? Or perhaps the medical press and the Ministry of Health might publicize the dangers attendant upon a hurried breakfast, a sprint for the train and long hours crushed with fellow-sufferers commuting to and from work?
> (Chisholm, 1964, pp. 12–13).

Since, as has been argued, we live in the world of the mind, it follows that the above problems can be seen as a battle for the mind. In this realm of persuasion and stimulation, it is the image which assumes the key role, and, in consequence, it is the image makers – the authors, controllers and disseminators of information – who hold a special responsibility. And it is the reasons and processes underlying the formation of particular interests and images that take on an especial significance.

9 Environmental Images, and Planning and Policy Implications II

The previous chapter, concerned with the regional images of 'north' and 'south' in the United Kingdom, demonstrated that such images could be of great importance in relation to public policy and planning. That 'the north' is seen unfavourably by key decision makers, such as industrialists, managers and civil servants, can act as a barrier to stimulating economic growth in the area. As a consequence various agencies promote a counter-image of 'the north', designed to produce a more favourable perception of the area by such people.

This example illustrates a more general point: the divergence, real or imagined, between images of both actual and desired urban and regional environments held by 'planners' (the sense in which this term is used is clarified below) and their various 'client' groups (those people whose behaviour planners attempt to influence or on whose lifestyles planning decisions have impact). A divergence between the viewpoints of planners and the planned for is now widely reported. Three far-flung examples will suffice. In the United Kingdom an assessment of the environment surrounding the home by an interdisciplinary team bore only 'limited resemblance' to the residents' view (Department of Environment, 1972). In the greater Detroit area there was 'considerable disagreement' between an architect–planner's assessment of neighbourhoods and that of residents'; on one question 88 per cent of people living in neighbourhoods professionally judged as unpleasant liked their neighbourhood at least moderately well (Lansing and Marans, 1969). In Sydney, Australia, there was a 'low correlation' between the professional and resident assessment; on one question 71 per cent of residents liked 'what they saw around' compared with a figure of 21 per cent for the professional assessment (Troy, 1971). Important issues arising from such consistent findings are the identification of those dimensions on which planners' images diverge from or converge with those of their clients, and the ability to measure these divergences and convergences. Image measurement methods have been suggested and used in this context and some examples of this approach are discussed in the following section.

Perhaps of more importance than identifying the degrees of agreement between planner and client images, are the actions taken by planners to increase agreement between various groups' environmental images. Broadly, these actions are of two types, used singly or in combination. The first are resource allocations that materially change the environment. Second, as demonstrated in the previous chapter, are the promotional and public relations methods designed to project the environmental images that will promote specific planning objectives (see also Gold, 1974). The success of this latter approach is dependent upon the transmission of information via the media and the processes of learning, whereby such information is accepted, ignored or rejected (some aspects of which were discussed in chapter 7). But to begin to grasp this more fully, as well as the key issue of why planners' images differ from those of their client groups, necessitates situating those issues in terms of wider social structures and relations, in terms of the role of planners as a social group. It is with such issues that the latter part of this chapter is concerned, taking up in a general way the question of the limits to solving planning problems at the subjective level by producing convergence between the images of environment held by various social groups.

DIVERGENT IMAGES AND IMAGE MEASUREMENT METHODS

In the previous chapter, the different images held by different people were revealed through textual analyses of written descriptions of the environment. However, this represents but one way of measuring images and in particular the more 'scientific', quantitative image measurement methods devised from the early 1960s have increasingly been used to measure the environmental images held by various groups of planners, environmental managers and their clients. Such methods have been applied in a variety of environmental contexts:

rural and recreational (Athoff and Greig, 1974; Baumann, 1969; Constantini and Hanf, 1972; Hendee and Harris, 1970; Sewell, 1971; although these are not a central concern here) as well as regional and urban (Appleyard, 1969; Donnelly *et al.*, 1973; Hudson 1976*b*; Lowenthal and Reil, 1972). The advent of such methods and approaches in planning might have been expected to produce a shift away from planning methodologies based on analogy with the behaviour of physical systems (for example Wilson, 1974) towards a more humane, individually oriented and sensitive planning philosophy and practice. The rationale generally given for such studies is aptly summed up by Craik:

> With the advent of massive urban renewal programs, the creation of entirely new communities, and the management of vast tracts of wilderness and parks, the relationship between professional designers, planners, and managers of the physical environment and their user-clients has become increasingly attenuated and indirect. There is a practical need for some new, reliable, empirical means of providing an understanding of client groups. At the same time, the sensibilities and possible preconceptions of professional groups also warrant study. Environmental design and management could proceed on a more enlightened basis if greater knowledge were available of the comprehensions of special user-client groups and special competence groups . . .
>
> (Craik, 1973, p. 85).

A rather different approach to this question of differing environmental images has been proposed by Kaplan (1973). Kaplan argues for the primacy of a theoretical approach in that only if an integrated model is made of how people construct their models of built environments can designers make use of the results of empirical investigations of images. He argues that man has a basic need for information, to interpret and make sense of this. As a consequence, the environment should be designed to meet this need offering both variety and uncertainty, permitting choice, but possessing a basic order so that sense can be made of it. This model has not been tested empirically. At another level, there are undertones of a social engineering approach to the relation of planning and image studies that some may find unsavoury.

Two recent British studies concerned with the environmental images of planners and their client groups have been undertaken in Sunderland (Donnelly *et al.*, 1973) and selected new towns (Hudson,

1976 *b*). The former was concerned with investigating the utility of perception studies and questionnaire methods to local authority planners. The interests were primarily methodological rather than aiming to provide substantive research results, involving initially a non-random sample of 150 people. Stressing the need for multi-method approaches, the authors investigated the utility of a variety of methods to study images of Sunderland and parts of the town: drawing sketch maps on to provided outline maps of the town; using photographs as stimuli; a number of questions designed to produce largely unstructured responses as to peoples' images of Sunderland and various perceived areas within the town. The authors point out that more sophisticated methods could have been used to measure images, such as the semantic differential technique or repertory grid methods, but that these are perhaps less suitable to the requirements of local authorities than the approach adopted.

Problems were nevertheless encountered with their chosen multi-method package. Respondents had problems in sketching local areas on to base maps, perhaps because of the paucity of information on these. However, this minimal information was intended to reduce the possible pre-structuring of respondents' images of the town. There were also problems in verbalising responses, particularly in relation to those areas in which people would like to live – a point of considerable methodological significance for the relationships of this type of research to planning. On the other hand, photographs were found to be a good tool in this research.

Over all, people in Sunderland were best able to grasp situations relating to their day-to-day experiences; much more difficulty was encountered in grasping more abstract notions. For example, most people were able to conceive of their local area but were less adept at grasping an image of Sunderland as a whole. To some degree these results echo the findings of Appleyard (1969) in a very different cultural and geographical setting (see below) and a similar pattern emerged in a study of images of northeastern New Towns (Hudson, 1976 *b*).

Hudson was concerned more with substantive than methodological issues, although the research had important methodological implications. The main concern of the research was the images of three New Towns in north-east England – Aycliffe, Peterlee and Washington – as held by their inhabitants and those responsible for the design and management of the towns. A random sample of 679 of the towns' inhabitants were interviewed and inhabitants' images measured using a variety of methods: primarily an attitude questionnaire but supplemented by unstructured tape-recorded interviews and repertory grids. The images of those responsible for the planning of the towns were measured less directly via a textual analysis of the towns' Master Plans, Annual Reports and promotional and public relations material issued by their Development Corporations.

While there were differences between the towns in the dimensions on which planners' and residents' images differed, in the dimensions on which various resident groups' images differed, and in the magnitude of such differences, certain generalisations can be validly drawn. On a whole range of issues to do with images of the regional roles of the towns or images of the towns as entities — industrial, housing, retail provision, social structure and relations — there was over-all marked consensus in the images of planners and residents. The towns were generally favourably perceived. However, when the level of resolution changed to residents' houses or local areas within the towns, considerable divergences in images emerged. While the planners' images remained favourable, those of the residents were more frequently critical. However, there were also differences between residents: in general unskilled manual workers were more critical of their immediate environments than those in white collar or professional occupations. The implications of this are important because the different environments experienced by various groups in the New Towns mainly reflect the resource allocation policies of their Development Corporations. More generally, material living conditions reflect planners' resource allocations. One needs to take account of these conditions and their determinants in considering divergence of images both between planners and their client groups and also between these various client groups.

While it is one thing to identify and measure such differences in images, it is by no means clear that such approaches will necessarily lead to better planning and resource allocation, in the sense of a more humane, individually-oriented planning practice and resource allocation. Put another way, what is at issue is what is meant by 'better' – who gains, who loses by such resource allocations. To begin to answer such a question and pursue the relation of environmental image studies to planning necessitates some consideration of planning as an activity and planners as a social group.

PLANNING, PLANNERS AND SOCIETY

Planning may be defined as resource allocation, taking a catholic view of resources to include location, mediated through the decisions of various branches of the State (compare Eversley, 1973). Planning is therefore conceived as something much wider than physical planning and the manipulation of spatial structure, although this is subsumed within the view of planning adopted here and it is recognised that social and economic structures also have a spatial expression. Crucially, planning generally involves resource allocation via methods other than those of the market and thus both presupposes and encompasses the formulation of goals and objectives and the rules for selecting courses of action to achieve these other than the dictates of the market. This in turn presupposes the existence of a value system which cannot find expression through the market. Planners are thus those members of the various branches of the State involved in taking such decisions (compare the notion of 'gatekeepers' proposed by Pahl, 1975).

Given this view of planning, it can currently be thought of as operating on one of two broad levels, depending on its relationship to wider social structures and relationships. Planning may be seen as an alternative to market forces as a resource allocation system: for example, as in the centralised resource allocation mechanisms of the USSR. Alternatively, and it is in this context that planning is viewed in the remainder of this chapter, planning may be seen as intervention within economies dominated by a capitalist mode of production, as in the United Kingdom. In such contexts planning is charged with a variety of tasks, such as the generation of economic growth via restructuring regional economies or key sectors of the economy, or the offsetting of the worst social impacts of the resource distribution generated by the dominant mode of production or maintaining or improving environmental quality. In other words, planning represents actions by the State fulfilling its role of factors of cohesion, designed to perpetuate and reproduce existing social relationships (Poulantzas, 1970).

Implicit in this latter view of the role of planning is that society is competitive, characterised by possibilities of class conflict that planning seeks to prevent. This is at variance with the image of society that tacitly underpins planning as generally conceived and planning as generally practised. In essence, this tacit image is that of a functionalist view of society that sees society as organised around a common set of values, possessing a common image of a desirable stable social state and tending towards such a stable state (see Parsons, 1951). Two issues arise here: the first is the implications of a competitive image of society for planning methods and practice; this aspect will be discussed in the next section. The second issue, which has implications for the first, is the sources of conflict in society. Rapoport (1974) suggests that there are three. Marxist theory puts resource allocation, the system of resource distribution corresponding to the dominant mode of production, which strongly influences the division of labour and class relations within society, at the heart of social conflict. The second source of conflict is the struggle for power, position and status – for the power of decision. As power often depends on control over capital, this question is closely allied to questions of economic control. A third source of conflict is the need for autonomy, for self-identification and identification of the self as part of a group. Implicitly, this is a 'them' and 'us' situation, a basic precondition for conflict which again relates back to the question of class relationships in society.

There is, therefore, a system of social relations whereby groups compete for resources (the precise expressions of competition varying from society to society). Such competition is usually, though not always, non-violent, regulated and legitimated by the laws and rules of a society. To explain the activities and environmental images of various social groups, including planners, it is necessary to examine these in the light of dominant social relations and structures. It is against this background that one can return to the differences in images held by planners and those whose behaviour planning attempts to influence, those whose behaviour is influenced by planning decisions.

IMPLICATIONS OF DIVERGENT IMAGES FOR PLANNING PHILOSOPHY AND METHODOLOGY

The recognition that planners as a social group possess environmental images that may differ from those whom they seek to influence or those who are affected by resource allocation decisions taken by planners raises some important issues. This does not deny that there is heterogeneity of viewpoints among planners both in the general sense and in relation to specific types of planner such as 'town planners'. Equally, other social groups differ in their viewpoints as was shown during the discussion of group images in chapter 5. The important point is that there is generally much greater internal agreement among planners than there is between planners and other social groups.

In order to determine the limits of 'solving' planning problems at the level of changing images, the material impacts of planning resource allocations are, for the moment, ignored. Rather, one can argue that different environmental images as held by planners and other social groups do not imply that one image is 'right', the other 'wrong'. Different groups construe environmental situations in different ways and it is open for them to change their constructions of reality. That is, the problem of different images (and by implication, resource allocation) could be 'solved' at this subjective level. But this raises the fundamental issue of deciding upon the desired image around which such a consensus could form, of deciding who is to take this decision. Three models of planning behaviour can be postulated, depending on how the definition of the desired environments is to be reached (see figure 9.1) and so on how one conceives of participation in the planning process (for some views on this, see Arnstein, 1969; Damer and Hague, 1971).

The first model of planning behaviour is that of 'the planner as leader'. This has been the dominant model in the United Kingdom, perhaps best exemplified by New Town planning, of which Thomas and Cresswell conclude:

> It is the planners' conception of reality which holds sway at least as a blueprint, and their clients, who may all along have wanted something else, who have to fit in as best they can.
>
> (Thomas and Cresswell, 1973, p. 50)

More generally it has been argued that traditionally planners have designed urban environments without consulting their user-clients (Porteous, 1971, p. 157). Participation, the relationship to the client, is defined as the latter reacting to proposals put forward by various planning agencies and authorities. This is epitomised by recent 'participation' exercises conducted in relation to the structure plan preparation in Great Britain and is closely linked to the use of questionnaire methodologies, the presentation of one or, at most, a

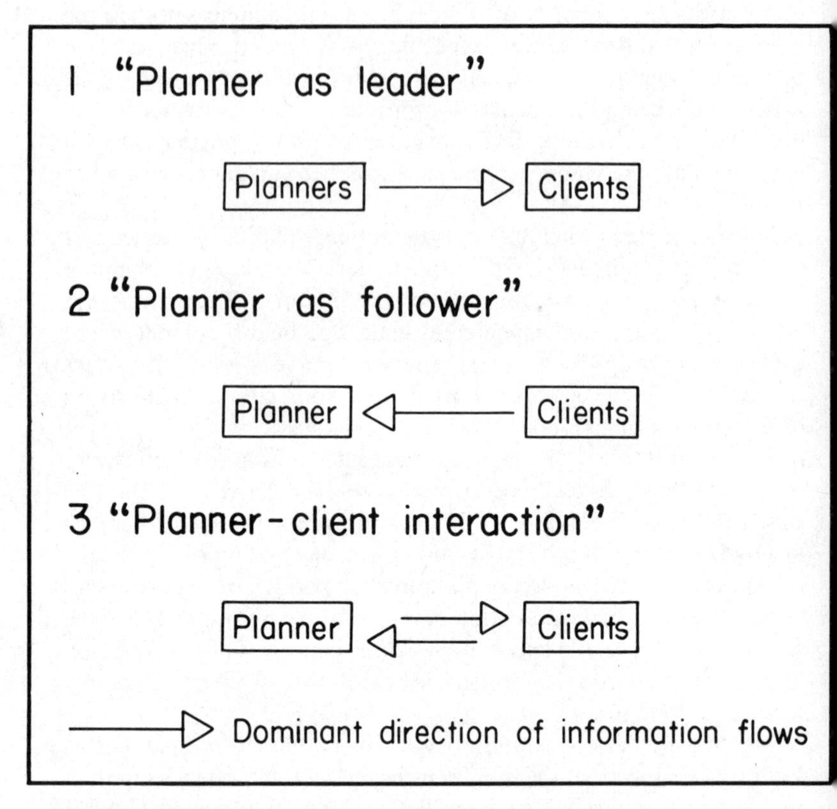

Figure 9.1 Models of planner – client relationships

few, alternative images of futures in the counties to which their population can respond, expressing their opinions on these narrowly prescribed range of scenarios. A technically more sophisticated and, in some ways, more realistic way of presenting alternative scenarios to people is the 'priority evaluator' whereby people express their desires as to future environments via a choice among a given set of possible environmental changes which can be made at given costs, subject to an overall budget constraint (see Hoinville, 1971).

One implication of this 'planner as leader' view of planning is that people must be educated or reeducated to accept a particular and, perhaps, different set of values and aspirations, a different image of the desirable environmental condition, to reconstrue reality in the same way as the planners. This is a view predicated on the assumption of the planner as the value-neutral, apolitical, technical expert, acting for the 'good of the community' or in the 'national interest', and one that is closely associated with the cult of the expert and the depoliticisation of planning. There are clear dangers of professional imperialism in this as an approach to planning; of the imposition of alien values and views of the world on unwilling recipients, often via advocating technical solutions to social problems.

A second model is to consider the obverse case, that of 'the planner as follower': that is, planners respond to the clients expressed needs, as seen by their clients (cf. Harvey, 1973). At a methodological level, such a position raises the problem of whether current tools are adequate to reveal images of desired environments. There is also the problem that needs are a social category that change over time, particularly in a society where, for example, advertising is universal and devoted to creating new demands for old and new commodities. More seriously, one can question whether it is sensible to attempt to ask people to define 'ideal' environments as people are heavily constrained by their range of experience when asked to construct alternative, more desirable, environments in which to live. Given current levels of technological development and the specialist skills these necessitate, strategic planning decisions on many key issues could not be taken via such an approach.

The idea of planners following their clients' expressed wishes is one that links to the idea of advocacy planning (see Goodman, 1972). Advocacy planning is based on the premise that radical planners work for deprived minority groups, representing their views to experts in various branches of the State and so enabling them more effectively to articulate their view-point within a pluralist, competitive society. The central weakness of this approach is that it depends on the definition of one group's needs by another and hence it fails to enable disadvantaged groups to help themselves. Thus it can easily fall into the trap of 'planner as leader' with its social engineering overtones.

The third model is based upon the premise of 'planner – client interaction': by which is meant a situation of the former explaining the reasons for their actions, and the latter conveying their needs as they see them to the planners. Thus, on the basis of a continuing dialogue, rather than consultation, a consensus emerges as to the 'best' course of action. There are formidable problems in adopting such a view. Besides problems of measurement and communication, such a view is idealistic in that it assumes planners wish to, and, more fundamentally, are able to serve the needs of their various client groups, regardless of power or status. To see why this is not the case requires viewing planning in the context of wider social structures and relations and in terms of the material impacts of resource allocations made by various planning agencies. This is taken up after the next section in which the conventional legitimations for the existence of divergent images between planners and other social groups are examined.

LEGITIMATION OF DIVERGENT IMAGES

It was pointed out above that the dominant model of planning in the United Kingdom (and similar societies) has been that of the 'planner as leader'. At the same time it has been widely acknowledged that there are wide differences in environmental images between planners and other client social groups. The existence of these differences and reactions to their existence is not unrelated to the dominance of the 'planner as leader' approach to planning.

It is argued by some that a combination of the methodological problems involved in eliciting peoples' needs or wishes as to future environments, coupled with the communications barriers resulting from the technical terms necessary in many aspects of planning, make it impossible to cater for the perceived needs of the majority. For example, Appleyard in analysing the planning of Ciudad Guayana, found many differences in the environmental images of the inhabitants and planners of the city, and went on to argue that:

> Urban populations are difficult to understand, inarticulate and anonymous, so that designers in a decision situation tend to fall back on their own perceptions and values supported by their professional stock of rules and models, and 'objective' data, often unaware of their dissociation from the other reality.

He continues:

> The current tools of city design, the land-use map and site plan, are poor descriptors of the city experience . . . designers therefore do not know of the effect of their plans on experience . . .
> (Appleyard, 1969, p. 422)

Thus Appleyard identifies the problem as a methodological and technical one: in essence, views built up from everyday experience of the environment, '. . . the other reality', are unlikely to correspond with those projected from planning documents.

Appleyard concludes that urban designers differ from urban dwellers on virtually all the variables relevant to images of the urban area, the very special knowledge and skills of the designer creating this gap. By virtue of their role and position urban planners have more knowledge and knowledge of a different type to that of the wider population, planners taking a broader, more abstract view less rooted in personal contact with and experience of the environment.

However, the reduction of the problem to a technical one begs several questions and is somewhat misdirected. It reflects an implicit conceptualisation of society as made up of two groups, planners and the rest, whereas in fact it is necessary to recognise that social structure and relations are much more subtle and complicated. In particular, it begs the question why—that is, in whose interests—certain types of knowledge are given primacy over others. This can most sensibly be answered by situating the production of knowledge in the context of social relations and class interests. The type of knowledge created for and by planners, cast in categories that tend to produce obfuscation and mystification, is created within and as part of an ideology whose aim is social control in the interests of powerful social groups. It is knowledge produced with a technical rather than an emancipatory interest (Habermas, 1972). In such a system it is imperative that technical knowledge be pre-eminent over that thrown up by the day-to-day experiences of the population which would suggest rather different patterns of social action from those favouring the interests of powerful groups.

PLANNING IN PRACTICE – UNEVEN RESOURCE ALLOCATION AND DIVERGENT IMAGES

Three models of resource allocation may be proposed: neutral allocation; progressive allocation; regressive allocation (see figure 9.2). The first of these, neutral allocation, may be quickly dismissed. To be viable, one of two conditions would have to hold. Firstly, there would be a consensus society. Secondly, planners as a social group could cut themselves off from wider social structures and relations

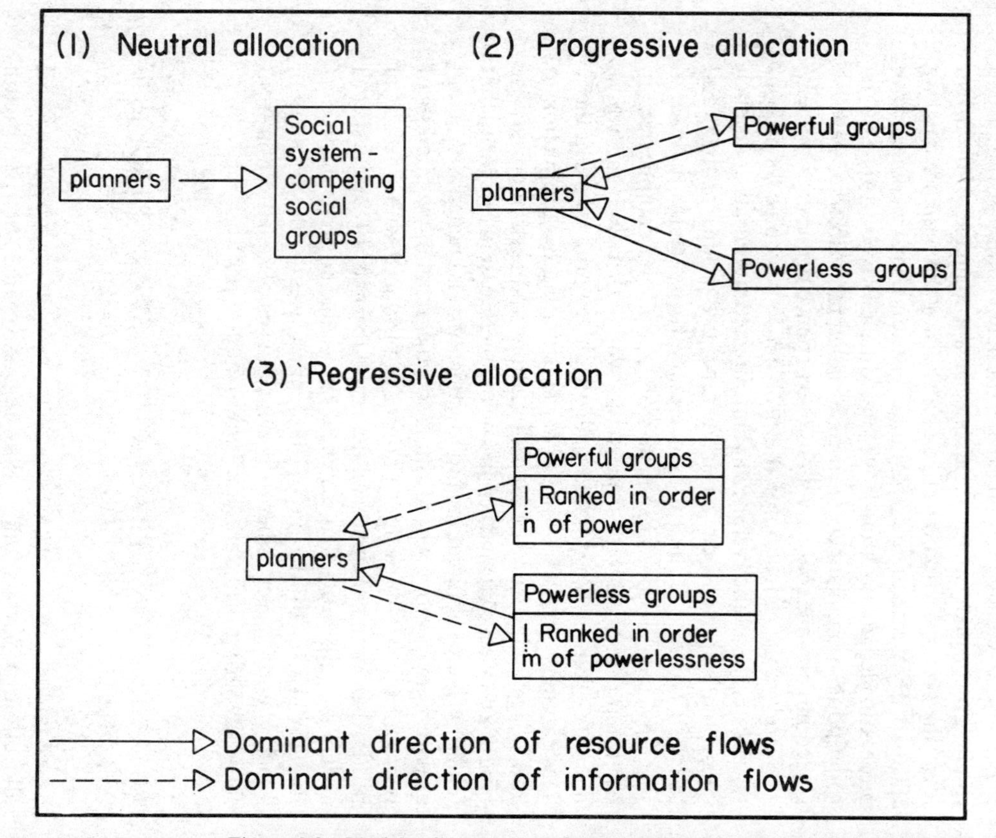
(1) Neutral allocation
planners
Social system - competing social groups
(2) Progressive allocation
planners
Powerful groups
Powerless groups
(3) Regressive allocation
planners
Powerful groups
Ranked in order of power
Powerless groups
Ranked in order of powerlessness
Dominant direction of resource flows
Dominant direction of information flows

and operate as an altruistic group, serving the whole community and the 'public interest'. However, this isolationist and idealist image is an untenable one. Planners *are* a social group (or groups), inextricably bound up in – indeed emerging in response to – existing social relationships, and planning as resource allocation reflects this structure.

The remaining two models of planning are progressive and regressive. In practice, planning through the State in various phases of capitalism encompasses both these elements: while the latter is dominant, the former is important in legitimating overall planning practices. Progressive planning entails allocation of resources from those in relatively advantaged positions to those in greater need: essentially, from rich to poor. Assuming that needs can be satisfactorily identified, resources are allocated in such a way as to counter the worst impacts of the distributive mechanisms of a capitalist mode of production. This implies that resources are allocated in a way that runs counter to the interests of at least some units of capital (although not the interests of the capital as a whole). This is to a degree true of some planning practices but two points remain to be made. First, there is a limit as to how far one can achieve redistribution without changes in the underlying structure of social relationships. Second, a degree of redistribution may be a necessary condition for the reproduction of existing patterns of social relationships.

The third possible model of resource allocation through planning sees allocation as a response to the imperatives of dominant social groups and, in a capitalist society, in the final analysis to the imperatives of capital. Planners also serve their own material self-interests – as a relatively powerful group – by such resource allocations. Planning, via the State apparatus, is seen as a form of social action that both mediates in class relations and serves the interests of powerful groups, widening rather than narrowing existing inequalities. It is important to realise that as well as the major qualitative differentiation in terms of their relation to capital between the two major social groups – 'powerful' and 'powerless' – there is a multitude of sub-groups within these major groups which have differing relative degrees of autonomy and ability to influence planners and compete for the resources that planners allocate. For example, while the major imperatives are those of private capital, it is nevertheless critical to appreciate that some 'powerless' groups wield far less bargaining power than do others: for example, unskilled manual workers are much less able to articulate their needs as they see them to urban planners than are middle management executives and this is reflected in their material living conditions.

At a variety of levels, then, planning acts not to narrow but to widen existing inequalities. But this widening of inequalities is not the result of a conspiracy of evil men so much as a necessary condition for the reproduction of existing social relations. However, the dominant image of planning is one of a progressive, at worst neutral, resource allocation system whereas the proposition put forward here is that the effects of planning in allocating resources are mainly regressive. An important question concerns the reasons why the image and reality of planning are so markedly different. To begin to understand why planning continues to be seen as socially progressive, it is necessary to consider the relationships between planning and ideology, a topic to which some planners have devoted attention (Planning Workshop, 1973). Ideologies both legitimate and provide a basic rationale for planning activity while virtually all planning begins from or contains ideological propositions – typically, in the case of town planning, those associated with an ideology of built-form determinism (Foley, 1960).

IDEOLOGY IN PLANNING AND PLANNING AS IDEOLOGY

Although ideologies are essentially 'world images', they have not been an issue of concern in most studies of urban and regional environmental images. This reflects certain characteristics of past and present environmental image studies: a lack of theoretical concern with why and from where images originate; a failure to set image studies in their social context and in the context of social and political structures, of which ideologies form a critical component. Thus, before moving on to consider the relationships between planning and ideology, a few words on ideologies *per se* are necessary. Ideologies, as already stated, represent 'world images', views of the world partly rooted in reality (Anderson, 1973). This partial rooting in reality is a necessary condition for such views to appear credible. For example, the element of progressive reformism associated with some planning policies is a necessary condition for the acceptance of an image of all of planning as progressive and reformist. But, nevertheless, ideologies significantly distort reality in such a way as to serve the sectional interests and legitimate the actions of certain groups, usually by presenting these as serving the interests of all groups: for example, as 'the public interest' or 'the national interest'. This is their essential characteristic.

Ideologies develop to serve the interests of various powerful groups in society; more generally, those of the ruling class. As representatives of ruling-class interests, ideologies become professionalised and institutionalised, and in late capitalism (see Mandel, 1975) the State comes to take on an increasing role in these processes, thus helping to reproduce these ideologies. While there are no simplistic formulae for discovering details of the production, reproduction and transformation of ideologies, it is important to make one elementary point. Orthodox social theory is produced by intellectuals in institutions embedded in wider societal structures. Such theory only gets transferred into concrete social situations, that is becomes ideology, when circumstances in society come to favour such a transfer. Ideologies can only be sensibly interpreted in terms of such circumstances, the material conditions in which they are partially rooted, for it is this characteristic that helps give these biased and self-interested views of reality their wider credibility. Consider, for example, Howard's (1898) vision of Garden Cities against the backcloth of nineteenth century urban England.

As the tenacity of Howard's vision of New Towns demonstrates, once established and serving the interests of powerful professions and groups (such as architects or urban managers) or the dominant class as a whole, ideologies are very tenacious and difficult to overthrow, partly because they tend to generate supportive social scientific knowledge. While they may be criticised at the level of ideas or theory, the overthrow of ideologies, as did their adoption, depends not simply on intellectual opposition but on wider forces within society.

Thus the role of ideologies is bound up with their nature and mode of (re)production: to legitimate social relationships, to rationalise or disguise inequality so as to preserve the favoured position of those who materially benefit from a particular pattern of social relationships. While based on and derived from the dominant mode and relationships of production, ideologies, once produced, take on an existence of their own and influence the images held by various social groups, generally with the purpose of legitimating social relationships from the viewpoint of those who materially benefit from these. If planners are viewed as a social group whose allocation decisions benefit those who already hold power, the links between these allocations and their legitimation are important. These relationships are considered further by means of an exemplary case study, that of the influence of State regional policies on economy and society in North-east England.

For some forty or so years, the image of the 'problems of the North-east' that has emerged from public policy and supportive intellectual documents has been remarkably consistent (Carney and Hudson, 1974). Essentially, this reduces to a proposition that because of exhaustion of resources, technological innovation and competition from other products and places, effective demand for the products of the region's traditional industries has declined. No attempt is made to analyse why effective demand declines; this is taken as an exogenous variable. As a result, the region now scores low on an arbitrarily selected battery of indicators, not only those directly related to the economic situation, such as unemployment rates and participation ratios, but also a variety of social and environmental indicators. It is through comparisons with the scores of other regions on such indicators that the problems of the region have been defined. As a result an image is projected of a region as 'lagging', 'backward', 'poor', 'declining' and so on (see chapter 8).

From this projected regional image and specification of the region's problems, certain policies emerge to 'solve' these 'problems'. The theme to consistently emerge is that of economic growth as the means to solve the problems of the region. Economic growth necessitates industrial growth and by promoting industrial growth it is asserted that the needs of people in the North-east can be best met. As the asserted cause of the condition of the region is its industrial structure, to attain industrial growth necessitates both structural and locational changes in the pattern of industry. But to 'modernise' the industrial structure in this way, attracting new industry to the region and restructuring that already present, requires providing the preconditions that would make such restructuring attractive to private capital: this means providing profitable locations for industry.

Thus policy advocates a whole series of changes in the region's people and environment to establish these preconditions.

People are told that they must change their social, cultural and industrial attitudes: to accept changing jobs and job skills as 'normal'. At the same time social capital in housing is concentrated into certain locations attractive to industry, thus helping build up suitable workforces and pools of labour by setting in motion inter- and intra-regional migration patterns. Paralleling the restructuring of housing provision, extensive restructuring of commercial property and transportation, especially road networks, has been set in motion to help provide environments attractive to industry. An essential component of this built environmental 'modernisation' – and so of the location of new industry – has been its locationally selective nature, based on a variety of coarse classifications of places in the North-east, classifications based upon the existing growth potential of these places. Places regarded as having growth potential have had public sector investment channelled to them; places perceived as lacking growth potential have been denied these resources.

The legitimation for setting in motion these widespread changes and encouraging uneven development within the region was to serve the needs of industry, given the assertion that these would coincide with those of the people of the region. That is, the gap between the North-east and other regions on the range of economic, social and environmental indicators that was defined as the 'regional problem' would be removed. However, the gap remains as wide as ever. Moreover, the apparent bankruptcy of public policy is admitted, perhaps unintentionally, from within policy (authors' emphasis):

> The region is paying its way. Regional policy has succeeded on almost every major front—*except employment and incomes.*
> (North of England Development Council, 1971)

Thus despite all the changes—social, economic and environmental—that have taken place in the North-east, despite the vigorous promotion of the counter-image (see chapter 8) and the attraction of industry, the problems remain. Even by their own criteria, existing policies and the theories that underpin them are self-confessedly bankrupt, their ideological nature becoming ever clearer. The assertion that the best way to meet the needs of people in the region is to meet the requirements of private capital is shown to be ideological; the changes set in motion benefit private capital at the expense of the vast majority of the people in the North-east.

CONCLUSION

This chapter and the previous one have examined some of the ways in which studies of urban and regional images can be of value in the planning process and in evaluating the nature of the planning process. By considering the different environmental images held by planners and other social groups, the reasons for the existence of such differences and the material impacts of resource allocations stemming from the planning process, the question of divergent images has been placed more firmly into its social context. A particularly important issue to emerge was that of the ideological nature of much planning activity, legitimating itself by asserting to serve the interests of all the people when in fact it can be shown to operate by serving particular sectional or class interests. Thus the environmental and world images projected by various planning agencies and bodies, the ideological nature and legitimating role of these images, are crucial to an understanding of the planning process at its various levels as mediated through the State.

10 Conclusion

As the urban environment becomes the home for an increasing number of people, there is an undeniable tendency for cities increasingly to resemble each other. The suburbs in particular are seen to project a uniformity and monotony. Although the road pattern may possess a geometry, there is a lack of both coherence and orientator-landmarks; although the dwelling units may differ, the variation is one of detail rather than recognised variety; the combined result is of confusion and monotony. Moreover, the general 'crime' of suburbia is that it blurs the distinction between town and country (Nairn, 1957), a feature originating in the anti-urbanism of the Victorian era, but without previous historical precedent and damaging to the city as an entity by encouraging 'place' to revert to 'space'. The 'insideness' becomes increasingly indistinguishable for the 'outsideness', such that the anonymous 'Anytown', for long the address shown on Post Office advertisements, becomes an increasingly familiar environment.

A uniformity of townscape in the most distinctive quarter, the city centre, has often resulted from the recent action of so-called city fathers. In seeking their own prestigious redevelopment schemes – in every instance replacing the vernacular or more human scale of an earlier wave of retail advance – the centres increasingly become essays in cubic commercialism, built of concrete or aluminium and glass. At ground level behind standardised fascias is offered standardised merchandise. Visually the scene is one of order, but one which has been 'simplified and cleaned up to such an extent that all it has to say is revealed at a glance' (Rapoport and Kantor, 1967, p. 211). This contrasts with the human predilection for a degree of variety, complexity and mystery. The 'cleaning-up' process can easily erase the individuality of place.

Standardised residential redevelopment in inner areas had led to an environmental deprivation, not least for children. High-rise dwellings, requiring children to be both silent and unseen, with stereotype ground-level play areas containing 'rungs to hop from like a pet bird'

(Rudofsky, 1969, p. 330), are anti-child environments, quite lacking in stimulus and challenge compared with the environments replaced (Eyken, 1967; Jacobs, 1961; Jephcott, 1971). They are without challenge, that is, unless it is considered that the very predictability of the environment has driven them to unpredictable, delinquent behaviour (Parr, 1965, p. 76; Rudofsky, 1969, pp. 330–3).

Even travel between places has been made more homogeneous, quite apart from the actual travel termini, whether motel, station or airport. Continuous-weld rails, diesel locomotion and air-conditioning have robbed rail travel of the sense of rhythm and speed, of noise and smell. Similarly, motorways, in erasing contours and widening the vision, have lost the 'feel' of the grain of a country which comes from a changing angle and perspective. Movement has been facilitated at the expense of the experience of travel.

Technology, which has led to the revaluation or destruction of distance, is similarly seen as the destroyer of the particularity of place. Scale changes in production and organisation have brought the diffusion of uniform materials and standardised designs. Even legislation drafted to safeguard environmental standards can be shown to have encouraged uniformity. This has been evident since the 1875 Public Health Act when ubiquitous standardisation followed legislation for minimum street width and distance between buildings; the same tendency is no less evident in the blind application of today's legislation on land-use zoning, development control and even internal space standards (Smith, 1972). A recent official document has, in fact, sought to dispel the notion that design standards are necessarily useful and show that the meeting of a standard can often harm the desired over-all result (Department of Environment, 1976).

The danger of an increasingly uniform environment is that it engages the individual in a less active perceptual response. The general consensus of researchers from a variety of disciplines, studying both human and animal habitat and behaviour, is that a complex environment is essential for optimum stimulation – for man's orientation, security and identity. Absence of such stimulation leads increasingly to environmental numbness and subliminal perception such that some researchers conclude man's survival as an urban animal may be a question, not of food or oxygen, but of his sanity (Neutra, 1969; Rapoport, 1974; Smith, 1974*c*). The planning and design of urban space is therefore more than an exercise in either physical standards or artistic embellishment.

At the outset there are those inherent qualities in physical form which have been present since man began: certain formal qualities derived from simple numerical relations based on the human figure and celestial bodies producing a cultural symbolism which has only recently been discarded. Particular arrangements of form and space, however humble, have always provoked particular responses, whether the cause be morphological (Cullen, 1961), functional (Appleton, 1975) or existential (Norberg-Schulz, 1965; 1971). The last author (1971, p. 103) has strongly attacked, as harmful to man's well-being, the present indulgence in 'a picturesque play with perceptual effects or in abstract combinatorial geometry' when there are principles underlying existential space which should be the basis for the 'concretised' architectural space.

If certain principles concerning built form emerge from a study of civilisation, in practice the accommodating of the rapidly increasing urban population in recent generations has been less than satisfactory. Without denying that room exists for educational enlightenment among the public, an understanding of the public's awareness, evaluations and preferences of place offer an obvious way of ultimately increasing satisfaction with place. Perception research has been carried out in three recognisable areas (Goodey, 1974*c*).

Image studies, following Lynch-type research strategies form the first, and earliest, exercises. Examples of use in planning exercises range from a 36-block urban renewal project in Kansas City (see Goodey, 1971, pp.25–6), to the new, multi-nuclei city of Ciudad Guayana in Venezula (Appleyard, 1969), to its use in the compilation of an official evaluation of the area covered in the South Hampshire Plan (1970).

Neighbourhood recognition or delimitation is a second area of perception research. Used extensively by academics, the most notable official survey was the 'home area' exercise incorporated in the Royal Commission on Local Government (1969) (see Community Attitudes Survey). This exercise itself, however, has proved to be no less an academic exercise. Moreover, a subsequent consultation document (Department of Environment, 1974) on neighbourhood councils made no mention of neighbourhood perception, nor of any part that such studies might play.

Environmental quality, citizens' evaluations and preferences have, again, been little used in officially organised surveys. A review of

American cities found six where image studies had been conducted, and in four of these there was no apparent connection between the studies and subsequent design and policy recommendations (Southworth and Southworth, 1973).

The approach of so-called 'likeability research' has advanced in recent years with the addition of field observation techniques, whereby citizens' behaviour is observed and analysed (Hall, 1966; Sommer, 1969) and inference of their preferences drawn. Such work, however, reports less on values, which are culturally-determined beliefs and desires, and more on needs, which are biologically-determined, and thus has affinity with the work of anthropologists and ethologists. Perception techniques themselves have become more sophisticated and rooted in psychological theory. Moreover, a diversity of techniques may now be applied to obtain the citizen's image, be it schoolchild (for example Spencer and Lloyd, 1974) or adult (for example Donnelly *et al.*, 1973). The latter study, a pioneer of its kind, sought both designative and appraisive information about the town – Sunderland – and its different quarters, including knowledge of 'access to power' and channels of communication. One factor to emerge was that behind the so-called apathy of the public lay a decided interest in the environment.

Image research studies as listed above must always be seen in the broader context of citizen participation and dominant patterns of social relationships, of democracy itself. Ultimately, therefore, the problem is one of learning and communication. While not operating in a social vacuum devoid of constraints on both ideas and actions, nevertheless, for planners there is the responsibility of making proposals and choices comprehensible to the public, and not mystifying through technical jargon or mathematisation. Whether it be a housing project, road plan, new industry or local government reorganisation, '*all* forms of information about our urban environment should be made understandable' (Wurman, 1971, p. 6). Again, the ideal should be a dialogue, rather than research strategy whereby alternatives are discussed and group consensus obtained. Whether the ideal is attainable, given present patterns of social relations, is debatable. The public, in turn, have no less a responsibility in this process of dialogue. One may wonder why children should learn Latin by rote but never learn to understand the environment through direct experience, except in the most perfunctory and unintegrated fashion. More generally, one may bewail with Rudofsky (1973) that 'the art of living is neither taught nor encouraged'.

This work began with several examples of ethnocentric perception, a pervasive phenomenon that caused the poet to plead:

> O wad some Pow'r the giftie gie us
> To see oursels as others see us.

Although we are unlikely to achieve such a state this side of eternity, the preceding chapters have sought to show how our patterns of knowledge are set in a sea of ignorance, and how preference may be a euphemism for prejudice. The quality of humility is a prerequisite of a humane environment.

Bibliography

ADAMS, J. S. (1969). Directional bias in intra-urban migration. *Econ. Geogr.*, **45**, 302–23.

ALLEN, J. L. (1976). Lands of myth, waters of wonder: the place of the imagination in the history of geographical exploration, in D. Lowenthal and M. J. Bowden (eds), *Geographies of the Mind*, Oxford University Press, London, pp. 41–60.

ALLPORT, G. W. (1954). *The Nature of Prejudice*, Beacon, Boston, Mass.

ALFHOFF, P. and GREIG, W. H. (1974). Environmental pollution control policy-making: an analysis of élite perceptions and preferences. *Envir. Behav.*, **6**, 259–98.

AMBROSE, P. (1969). *Analytical Human Geography*, Longmans, London.

ANDERSON, J. (1971). Space – time budgets and activity studies in urban geography and planning. *Envir. Behav.*, **3**, 353–69.

ANDERSON, J. (1973). Ideology in geography: an introduction. *Antipode*, **5**, 1–6.

ANDERSON, J. and TINDALL, M. (1972). The concept of home range: new data for the study of territorial behaviour. *Environmental Design Research Association*, **3**, sections 1.1–7.

ANDREWS, H. F. (1973). Home range and urban knowledge of school-age children. *Envir. Behav.*, **5**, 73–86.

APPLETON, J. (1975). *The Experience of Landscape*, Wiley, London.

APPLEYARD, D. (1969). City designers and the pluralistic city, in L. Rodwin (ed.), *Urban Growth and Regional Development*, M.I.T. Press, Cambridge, Mass., pp. 422–52.

APPLEYARD, D. (1970*a*). Styles and methods of structuring a city. *Envir. Behav.*, **2**, 100–17.

APPLEYARD, D. (1970*b*). Notes on urban perception and knowledge, in J. Archea and C. Eastman (eds), *E. D. R. A. 2: Proceedings of Second Annual Environmental Design Research Association Conference*, Dowden, Hutchinson and Ross, Stroudsburg, Penn.,

pp. 97–101.
APPLEYARD, D., LYNCH, K. and MYER, J. (1964). *The View from the Road,* M.I.T. Press, Cambridge, Mass.
ARCHEA, J. and EASTMAN, C. (eds) (1970). *E. D. R. A. 2: Proceedings of Second Annual Environmental Design Research Association Conference*, Dowden, Hutchinson and Ross, Stroudsburg, Pennsylvania.
ARDREY, R. (1967). *The Territorial Imperative,* Collins, London.
ARNSTEIN, S. R. (1969). A ladder of citizen participation. *J. Am. Inst. Plann.,* **35,** 216–24.
ATTNEAVE, F. H. (1954). Some informative aspects of visual perception. *Psychol. Rev.,* **61,** 183–93.
BARRELL, J. (1972). *The Idea of Landscape and the Sense of Place, 1730–1840,* Cambridge University Press, Cambridge.
BATEMAN, M., BURTENSHAW, D. and DUFFETT, A. (1974). Environmental perception and migration: a study of perception of residential areas in South Hampshire, in D. Canter and T. Lee (eds), *Psychology and the Built Environment,* Architectural Press, London, pp. 148–55.
BAUMANN, D. (1969). The recreational use of domestic water supply reservoirs: perception and choice. University of Chicago Department of Geography, *Research Paper,* No. 121.
BEAZLEY, C. R. (1949). *The Dawn of Modern Geography,* vol. 2, Peter Smith, New York.
BENNETT, A. (1902). *Anna of the Five Towns,* Chatto & Windus, London.
BENTLEY, P. (1941). *The English Regional Novel,* Allen & Unwin, London.
BERLYNE, D. E. (1962). Uncertainty and epistemic curiosity. *Br. J. Psychol.,* **53,** 27–35.
BERLYNE, D. E. (1963). Motivational problems raised by exploratory and epistemic behaviour, in S. Koch (ed.), *Psychology: Study of a Science*, McGraw-Hill, New York.
BERNSTEIN, B. (1971). *Class, Codes and Control,* Routledge and Kegan Paul, London.
BERRY, B. J. L. (1964). Approaches to regional analysis: a synthesis. *Ann. Ass. Am. Geogr.,* **54,** 2–11.
BERRY, B. J. L. (1970). The geography of the United States in the year 2000. *Trans. Inst. Br. Geogr.,* **51,** 21–53.
BISHOP, J. and FOULSHAM, J. (1973). Children's images of

Harwich. *Working Paper,* no. 3, Architectural Psychology Research Unit, Kingston Polytechnic.

BLACKBOURN, A. (1973). Locational decisions in the international corporation. *Proc. Ass. Am. Geogr.,* **5,** 22–4.

BLAUT, J. M., McCLEARY, G. M. and BLAUT, A. S. (1970). Environmental mapping in young children. *Envir. Behav.,* **2,** 335–49.

BLOWERS, A. (1973). The neighbourhood: exploration of a concept, in *The City as a Social System,* The Open University, Social Sciences, block 2, pp. 49–94.

BOAL, F. (1969). Territoriality on the Shankhill – Falls divide, Belfast. *Ir. Geogr.,* **6,** 33–4, 41.

BOGDANOVIC, (1975). Symbols in the city and the city as symbol. *Ekistics,* **39,** 140–6.

BOULDING, K. E. (1956). *The Image,* University of Michigan Press, Ann Arbor.

BRAINE, J. (1957). *Room at the Top,* Eyre & Spottiswoode, London.

BRAINE, J. (1976). *Waiting for Sheila,* Eyre & Methuen, London.

BRANDWOOD, G. (1968). Schoolchildren's view of Britain, in J. P. Cole (ed.), *Bulletin of Quantitative Data for Geographers,* **18,** pp. 8–12.

BRENNAN, T. (1948). *Midland City,* Dobson, London.

BRIDGMAN, P. (1959). *The Way Things Are,* Harvard University Press, Cambridge.

BRIGGS, A. (1963). *Victorian Cities,* Odhams, London.

BRIGGS, A. (1970). The sense of place, in Smithsonian Institute, *The Fitness of Man's Environment,* Smithsonian Institute Press, Washington, pp. 77–98.

BRIGGS, R. (1973). Urban cognitive distance, in R. Downs and D. Stea (eds), *Image and Environment,* Aldine, Chicago, pp. 361–88.

BRILL, E. J. (ed.) (1967). *Urban Core and Inner City,* University of Leiden.

BRITISH STEEL CORPORATION (1972). *Report on B.S.C. Proposed Complex at Redcar,* London.

BROADY, M. (1968). *Planning for People,* National Council of Social Service, London.

BRONTË, E. (1847). *Wuthering Heights,* Arnold, London, 1964 edition.

BROWN, L. A. and MOORE, E. G. (1969). Diffusion research in geography: a perspective, in C. Board, R. J. Chorley, P. Haggett and D. Stoddart (eds), *Progr. Geogr.*, **1,** 119–57.

BROWN, L. A. and MOORE, E. G. (1970). The intra-urban migration process: a perspective. *Geogr. Annlr,* Series B, **52,** 1–13.

BRUNER, J. S. (1951). Personality dynamics and the process of perceiving, in R. R. Blake and G. V. Ramsey (eds), *Perception: An Approach to Personality,* Ronald, New York, pp. 121–47.

BULMER, M. (ed.) (1975). *Working Class Images of Society,* Routledge & Kegan Paul, London.

BURGESS, J. A. (1974). Stereotypes and urban images. *Area,* **6,** 167–71.

BURTON, I. (1963). The quantitative revolution and theoretical geography. *Can. Geogr.*, **7,** 151–62.

BUSINESS DECISIONS LTD (1974). *Industrial and Commercial Development: Summary of Research Findings.*

BUTTIMER, A. (1969). Social space in interdisciplinary perspective. *Geogr. Rev.* **59,** 417–26.

CANTER, D. V. (1974). *Psychology for Architects,* Applied Science, London.

CANTER, D. V. (1975). Distance estimation in Greater London. *S. S. R. C. Final Report,* University of Surrey.

CANTER, D. V. (ed.) (1975). *Environmental Interaction,* Surrey University Press.

CANTER, D. and LEE, T. (eds) (1974). *Psychology and the Built Environment*, Architectural Press, London.

CANTER, D. V. and TAGG, S. K. (1975). Distance estimation in cities. *Envir. Behav.*, **7,** 59–80.

CANTER, D. and WOOLS, R. (1970). A technique for the subjective appraisal of buildings. *Bldg Sci.*, **5,** 187–98.

CARNEY, J. G. and HUDSON, R. (1974). Ideology, public policy and underdevelopment in the North East. North East Area Study, *Working Paper,* No. 6, University of Durham.

CARR, S. and SCHISSLER, D. (1969). The city as a trip: perceptual selection and memory in the view from the road. *Envir. Behav.*, **1,** 7–35.

CHERMAYEFF, S. and ALEXANDER, C. (1966). *Community and Privacy,* Penguin, London.

CHESTERTON, G. K. (1901). A defence of detective stories. *Defendant,* 158–9.

CHISHOLM, M. (1964). Must we all live in South-east England? The location of new employment. *Geography,* **49,** 1–14.

CHISHOLM, M. (1966). *Geography and Economics,* Bell, London.

CHRISTALLER, W. (1966). *Central Places in Southern Germany,* C. W. Baskin (trans.), Prentice Hall, Englewood Cliffs.

COATES, B. E. and RAWSTRON, E. M. (1971). *Regional Variations in Britain: Studies in Economics and Social Geography,* Batsford, London.

COLE, J. P. (1959). *Geography of World Affairs,* Penguin, Harmondsworth.

COLE, J. P. (1972). A Mexican view of Britain. *Ideas in Geography,* **45,** Department of Geography, University of Nottingham.

COMMUNITY ATTITUDES SURVEY: ENGLAND (1969). *Research Studies,* **9,** for Royal Commission on Local Government in England, H.M.S.O., London.

COMMUNITY SURVEY: SCOTLAND (1969). *Research Studies,* **2,** for Royal Commission on Local Government in Scotland, H.M.S.O., London.

CONSTANTINI, E. and HANF, K. (1972). Environmental concern and Lake Tahoe: a study of élite perceptions, backgrounds and attitudes. *Envir. Behav.,* **4,** 209–42.

COOKE, A. (1975). *The American in England,* Cambridge University Press, Cambridge.

COOPER, C. (1972). The house as symbol. *Design Envir.,* **3,** 30–7.

COOPER, C. (1974). The house as symbol of the self, in J. Lang *et al.,* (eds), *Designing for Human Behaviour,* Dowden, Hutchinson & Ross, Stroudsburg, pp. 130–46.

COX, H. G. (1965). *The Secular City,* Student Christian Movement, London.

COX, K. R. (1966). The application of linear programming to geographical problems. *Tijdschr. econ. soc. Geogr.,* **56,** 228–36.

CRAIK, K. H. (1968). The comprehension of the everyday physical environment. *J. Am. Inst. Plann.,* **34,** 29–37.

CRAIK, K. H. (1970). Environmental psychology. *New Direct. Psychol.,* **4,** 1–121.

CRAIK, K. H. (1971). The assessment of places, in P. McReynolds (ed.), *Advances in Psychological Assessment,* vol. 2, Science & Behavior Books, Palo Alto.

CULLEN, G. (1961). *Townscape,* Architectural Press, London.

CURRY, L. (1962). Climatic change as a random series. *Ann. Ass.*

Am. Geogr., **52,** 21–31.

DAMER, S. and HAGUE, C. (1971). Public participation in planning: a review. *Tn. Plann. Rev.*, **42,** 217–32.

DENNIS, W. (1951). Cultural and developmental factors in perception, in R. R. Blake and G. V. Ramsey (eds), *Perception: An Approach to Personality,* Ronald, New York, pp. 148–69.

DEPARTMENT OF ENVIRONMENT (1972). *Estate Outside the Dwelling,* Design Bulletin, 25, H.M.S.O., London.

DEPARTMENT OF ENVIRONMENT (1974). *Neighbourhood Councils in England,* Consultation Paper, H.M.S.O., London.

DEPARTMENT OF ENVIRONMENT (1976). *The Value of Standards for the External Residential Environment,* Research Report, 6, H.M.S.O., London.

DERRICK, E. and McRORY, J. (1973). Cup in hand: Sunderland's self-image after the cup. *Working Paper,* 8, Centre for Urban & Regional Studies, University of Birmingham.

DICKENS, C. (1854). *Hard Times;* edition by Hazell, Watson & Viney, London.

DOHERTY, J. M. (1968). Residential preferences for urban environments in the United States. *Discussion Paper,* 29, Graduate School of Geography, London School of Economics.

DONNELLY, D., GOODEY, B. and MENZIES, M. (1973). Perception-related survey for local authorities: a pilot survey in Sunderland. *Research Memorandum,* 20, Centre for Urban & Regional Studies, University of Birmingham.

DONNELLY, D. and MENZIES, M. (1973). Meaning in imagery: the role of personal construct theory. *Working Paper,* 2, Centre for Urban & Regional Studies, University of Birmingham.

DOWNS, R. (1970*a*). The cognitive structure of an urban shopping centre. *Envir. Behav.*, **2,** 13–39.

DOWNS, R. (1970*b*). Geographic space perception: past approaches and future prospects. *Progr. Geogr.*, **2,** 65–108.

DOWNS, R. and STEA, D. (eds) (1973). *Image and Environment,* Aldine, Chicago.

DOYLE, A. CONAN (1888). On the geographical distribution of British intellect. *The Nineteenth Century,* pp. 184–95.

DURRELL, L. (1969). *Spirit of Place: Letters and Essays on Travel,* Faber and Faber, London.

DYOS, H. J. and WOLFF, M. (1973). *The Victorian City: Images and Reality,* Routledge & Kegan Paul, London.

ELLIS, B. (1966). *Basic Concepts of Measurement,* Cambridge University Press, Cambridge.

ENGLISH TOURIST BOARD (1974). *English Holidays: Official Guide to the Eleven Faces of England,* London.

EVERSLEY, D. E. C. (1973). *The Planner in Society,* Faber, London.

EYKEN, V. DER (1967). *The Pre-School Years,* Penguin, Harmondsworth.

EYLES, J. D. (1968). Inhabitants' images of Highgate Village (London). *Discussion Paper 15,* Graduate School of Geography, London School of Economics.

FABER, R. (1976). *French and English,* Faber, London.

FISHER, G. H. (1971–3). Perceptual maps of Newcastle-upon-Tyne (1971), Cardiff (1972), Durham (1972), York (1973).

FOLEY, D. L. (1960). British town planning: one ideology or three? *Br. J. Sociol.,* **2,** 211–31.

FRANCESCATO, D. and MEBANE, W. (1973). How citizens view two great cities: Milan and Rome, in R. Downs and D. Stea (eds), *Image and Environment,* Aldine, Chicago, pp. 131–47.

FRANK, L. K. (1948). *Society as the Patient,* Rutgers, New Brunswick.

FRIED, M. (1963). Grieving for a lost home: psychological costs of relocation, in L. J. Duhl (ed.), *The Urban Condition,* Basic Books, New York.

GANS, H. J. (1962). *The Urban Villagers: Group and Class in the Life of Italian-Americans,* Free Press, New York.

GANS, H. J. (1972) *People and Plans*, Penguin, Harmondsworth.

GARNER, B. J. (1968). The analysis of qualitative data in urban geography: the example of shop quality, in Inst. Br. Geogr., Study Group in Urban Geography, *Techniques in Urban Geography,* pp. 16–30.

GIBSON, E. J. (1970). The development of perception as an adaptive process. *Am. Scient.,* **58,** 98–107.

GIBSON, J. J. (1950). *The Perception of the Visual World,* Houghton Mifflin, Boston.

GIDDENS, A. (1976). *New Rules of Sociological Method*, Hutchinson, London.

GILBERT, E. W. (1960). The idea of the region. *Geography,* **45,** 157–75.

GLENROTHES DEVELOPMENT CORPORATION (1963). Comparison of the climate of the coastal area of Fife with that of the county of Kent. *Glenrothes for Industry*, Appendix C.

GODDARD, J. B. (1971*a*). Office communications and office location: a review of current research. *Reg. Stud.*, **5**, 263–80.

GODDARD, J. B. (1971*b*). Residential desirability of some British towns. Unpublished survey for Geographical Association.

GOLD, J. R. (1974). Communicating images of the environment. Centre for Urban and Regional Studies *Occasional Paper* No.29, University of Birmingham.

GOLLEDGE, R. G. (1967). Conceptualising the market decision process. *J. reg. Sci.*, **7**, (Supplement) 239–58.

GOLLEDGE, R. G. (1969). The geographical relevance of some learning theories, in K. R. Cox and R. G. Golledge (eds), Behavioural problems in geography: a symposium. *Northwestern University Studies in Geography*, No. 17, Evanston, Illinois, pp. 101–45.

GOLLEDGE, R. G., BRIGGS, R. and DEMKO, D. (1969). The configuration of distances in intra-urban space. *Proc. Ass. Am. Geogr.* **1**, 60–6.

GOLLEDGE, R. G. and ZANNARAS, G. (1970). The perception of urban structure: an experimental approach, in J. Archea and C. Eastman (eds), *EDRA 2, Proceedings of Second Annual Conference*, Carnegie Press, Pittsburgh.

GOLLEDGE, R. G. and ZANNARAS, G. (1973). Cognitive approaches to the analysis of human spatial behaviour, in W. H. Ittleson (ed.), *Environment and Cognition*, Seminar Press, New York, pp. 59–94.

GOODCHILD, B. (1974). Class differences in environmental perception. *Urban Stud.*, **11**, 157–69.

GOODEY, B. (1971). Perception of the environment. *Occasional Paper*, 17, Centre for Urban and Regional Studies, University of Birmingham.

GOODEY, B. (1974*a*). *Where You're At*, Penguin, Harmondsworth.

GOODEY, B. (1974*b*). Regional and urban images in decision making and planning, in J. Rees and P. Newby (eds), Behavioural perspectives in geography. *Middlesex Polytechnic Monographs in Geography*, No. 1, pp. 59–80.

GOODEY, B. (1974*c*). Images of place: essays on environmental perception, communications and education. *Occasional Paper*, 30,

Centre for Urban & Regional Studies, University of Birmingham.
GOODEY, B., DUFFETT, A. W., GOLD, J. R. and SPENCER, D. (1971). City scene: an exploration into the image of Central Birmingham. *Research Memorandum,* 10, Centre for Urban & Regional Studies, University of Birmingham.
GOODEY, B. and LEE, S. A. (1971). *The City Scope Project, Hull 1971,* Report for McKinsey & Co., London.
GOODMAN, P. (1969). *New Reformation,* Random House, New York.
GOODMAN, R. (1972). *After the Planners,* Penguin, Harmondsworth.
GOULD, P. R. (1965). Wheat on Kilimanjaro: the perception of choice within game and learning model frameworks. *General Systems,* **1,** 157–66.
GOULD, P. R. (1966). On mental maps, in R. Downs and D. Stea (eds) (1973). *Image and Environment,* Aldine, Chicago, pp. 182–220.
GOULD, P. R. (1973). The black boxes of Jönköping: spatial information and preference, in Downs and Stea, (eds), *Image and Environment,* Aldine, Chicago, pp. 234–45.
GOULD, P. and WHITE, R. (1968). The mental maps of British school-leavers. *Reg. Stud.,* **2,** 161–82.
GOULD, P. and WHITE, R. (1974). *Mental Maps,* Penguin, Harmondsworth.
GUELKE, L. (1971). Problems of scientific explanation in geography. *Can. Geogr.* 15, 38–53.
HABERMAS, J. (1972). *Knowledge and Human Interests*, Heinemann, London.
HÄGERSTRAND, T. (1968). *Innovation Diffusion as a Spatial Process,* University of Chicago Press, Chicago.
HALL, E. T. (1966). *The Hidden Dimension,* Doubleday, New York.
HALL, J. M. (1970). Industry grows where the grass is greener. *Area,* **3,** 40–6.
HARRIS, C. (1971). Theory and synthesis in historical geography. *Can. Geogr.,* **15,** 157–72.
HARRIS, M. (1973). *The Dilly Boys: Male Prostitution in Piccadilly,* Croom Helm, London.
HARRISON, J. and HOWARD, W. (1972). The role of meaning in the urban image. *Envir.Behav.,* **4,** 389–411.
HARRISON, J. A. and SARRE, P. (1971). Personal construct

theory in the measurement of environmental images: problems and methods. *Envir. Behav.,* **3,** 351–74.

HARRISON, J. A. and SARRE, P. (1975). Personal construct theory in the measurement of environmental image. *Envir. Behav.,* **7,** 3–58.

HART, J. T. (1971). The inverse care law. *The Lancet,* 405–12.

HART, R. A. and MOORE, G. T. (1973). The development of spatial cognition: a review, in R. Downs and D. Stea (eds), *Image and Environment,* Aldine, Chicago, pp. 246–88.

HARVEY, D. W. (1967). The problems of theory construction in geography. *J. reg. Sci.,* **7,** (Supplement), 211–16.

HARVEY, D. W. (1969*a*). *Explanation in Geography,* Arnold, London.

HARVEY, D. W. (1969*b*). Conceptual and measurement problems in the cognitive-behavioural approach to location theory, in K. R. Cox and R. G. Golledge (eds), Behavioural problems in geography. *Northwestern University Studies in Geography,* No. 17, Evanston, Illinois.

HARVEY, D. W. (1973). *Social Justice and the City,* Arnold, London.

HEATHCOTE, R. (1965). *Back of Bourke: A Study of Land Approval and Settlement in Semi-Arid Australia,* University Press, Melbourne.

HENDEE, J. C. and HARRIS, R. W. (1970). Foresters' perceptions of wilderness-user attitudes and perceptions. *J. Forest.,* **68,** 759–62.

HERBERT, D. T. (1973). Residential mobility and preference: a study of Swansea, in B. D. Clark and M. B. Gleave, *Social Patterns in Cities, Inst. Br. Geogr.,* Special Publication, 5.

HERSCHBERGER, R. G. (1968). A study of meaning in architecture. *Man and his Environment,* **1,** 6–7.

HERSCHBERGER, R. G. (1972). Toward a set of semantic scales to measure the meaning of architectural environments, in W. J. Mitchell (ed), *Environmental Design Research 3,* vol. 1, Dowden, Hutchinson & Ross, Stroudsburg, sections 6–4–1 to 10.

HICKS, E. P. and BEYER, B. K. (1968). Images of Africa. *Social Educ.,* **32,** 779–84.

HOINVILLE, G. (1971). Evaluating community preferences. *Envir. Plann.,* **3,** 33–50.

HONOUR, H. (1976). *The New Golden Land, European Images of*

America from the Discoveries to the Present Time, Allen Lane, London.
HORTON, F. and REYNOLDS, D. R. (1970). Intra-urban migration and the perception of residential quality. Department of Geography, *Research Paper,* 13, Ohio State University, Columbus.
HORTON, F. and REYNOLDS, D. R. (1971). Effects of urban spatial structure on individual behaviour. *Econ. Geogr.,* **47,** 36–48.
HOUSE, J. W. *et al.* (1968). Mobility of the northern business manager. *Papers on Migration and Mobility in Northern England,* 8, University of Newcastle.
HOWARD, E. (1898) *Tomorrow: a Peace Path to Real Reform;* revised edition, *Garden Cities of Tomorrow* (1902); reprint edited by F. J. Osborn (1965), Faber & Faber, London.
HUDSON, R. (1974*a*). Consumer Spatial Behaviour: A Conceptual Model and Empirical Investigation in Bristol. Unpublished Ph.D. thesis, University of Bristol.
HUDSON, R. (1974*b*). Images of the retailing environment: an example of the use of the repertory grid methodology. *Envir. Behav.,* **6,** 470–94.
HUDSON, R. (1975). Patterns of spatial search. *Trans. Inst. Br. Geogr.,* **65,** 141–54.
HUDSON, R. (1976*a*). Linking studies of the individual with models of aggregate behaviour: an empirical example. *Trans. Inst. Br. Geogr.,* **1** (New Series), 159–74.
HUDSON, R. (1976*b*). *New Towns in North East England* (2 vols.), North East Area Study, University of Durham.
HUFF, D. L. (1960). A topographical model of consumer space preferences. *Pap. Proc. reg. sci. Ass.,* **7,** 159–73.
HULL, C. L. (1943). *Principles of Behaviour,* Appleton-Century-Crofts, New York.
HULL, C. L. (1951). *Essentials of Behaviour,* Appleton-Century-Crofts, New York.
HULL, C. L. (1952). *A Behaviour System,* Yale University Press, New Haven.
ISARD, W. (1956). *Location the Space-Economy,* M.I.T. Press, Cambridge, Mass.
ISARD, W. (1960). *Methods of Regional Analysis,* M.I.T. Press, Cambridge, Mass.
ITTELSON, W. H. (1960). *Visual Space Perception,* Springer, New

York.

ITTELSON, W. H. (ed.) (1973). *Environment and Cognition,* Seminar Press, New York.

JACKSON, L. E. and JOHNSTON, R. J. (1972). Structuring the image: an investigation of the elements of mental maps. *Envir. Plann.,* **4,** 415–27.

JACOBS, J. (1961). *The Death and Life of Great American Cities,* Random House, New York.

JEPHCOTT, P. (1971). Homes in high flats. University of Glasgow, Social & Economic Studies, *Occasional Papers,* 13.

JOHNS, E. (1965). *British Townscapes,* Arnold, London.

JOHNS, E. (1971). Symmetry and asymmetry in the urban scene. *Area,* **2,** 48–57.

JOHNSTON, R. J. (1970). Latent migration potential and the gravity model: a New Zealand study. *Geogr. Analysis,* **2,** 387–97.

JOHNSTON, R. J. (1971). Mental maps of the city: suburban preference patterns. *Envir. Plann.,* **3,** 63–71.

JOHNSTON, R. J. (1972). Activity spaces and residential preference: some tests of the hypothesis of sectoral mental maps. *Econ. Geogr.,* **48,** 199–211.

JONGE, D. DE (1962). Images of urban areas: their structure of psychological foundations. *J. Am. Inst. Plann.,* **28,** 266–76.

KANE, J. N. and ALEXANDER, G. L. (1965). *Nicknames of Cities and States of the United States,* Scarecrow, New York.

KAPLAN, S. (1973). Cognitive maps in perception and thought, in R. Downs and D. Stea (eds), *Image and Environment,* Aldine, Chicago, pp. 63–78.

KASMAR, J. V. (1970). The development of a usable lexicon of environmental descriptors. *Envir. Behav.,* **2,** 153–69.

KATONA, G. (1951). *Psychological Analysis of Economic Behaviour,* McGraw-Hill, New York.

KEEBLE, D. E. (1971). Employment mobility in Britain, in M. D. I. Chisholm and G. Manners (eds), *Spatial Policy Problems of the British Economy* University Press, Cambridge.

KELLY, G. A. (1955). *The Psychology of Personal Constructs,* vols. 1 and 2, Norton, New York.

KIRK, W. (1951). Historical geography and the concept of the behavioural environment. *Indian Geogr. J., Silver Jubilee Edition,* 152–60.

KLEIN, H. J. (1967). The delimitation of the town centre in the image of its citizens, in E. J. Brill (ed.), *Urban Core and Inner City,* University of Leiden, pp. 286–306.

KNOEPFLMACHER, U. C. (1973). The novel between city and country, in H. J. Dyos and M. Wolff, *The Victorian City: Images and Reality,* Routledge & Kegan Paul, London, pp. 517–36.

KOFFKA, K. (1935). *Principles of Gestalt Psychology,* Kegan Paul, Tench, Trubner, New York.

KOHLER, W. (1947). *Gestalt Psychology,* Liveright, New York.

LADD, F. C. (1970). Black youths view their environment: neighbourhood maps. *Envir. Behav.,* **2,** 74–99.

LADD, F. C. (1972). Black youths view their environment: some views of housing. *J. Am. Inst. Plann.,* **38,** 108–17.

LANG, J., BURNETTE, C., MOLESKI, W., VACHON, D. (eds) (1974). *Designing for Human Behaviour,* Dowden, Hutchinson & Ross, Stroudsburg.

LANGER, S. K. (1953). *Feeling and Form,* Routledge & Kegan Paul, London.

LANSING, J. B. and MARANS, W. W. (1969). Evaluation of neighbourhood quality. *J. Am. Inst. Plann.,* **35,** 195–9.

LASLETT, P. (1968). *The World We Have Lost,* Methuen, London.

LAWRENCE, D. H. (1915). *The Rainbow,* Penguin, Harmondsworth, 1949.

LAWRENCE, D. H. (1924). *Studies in Classic American Literature,* Martin Secker, London (1933 edition).

LAWRENCE, D. H. (1929). Nottingham and the mining country, in *Selected Essays,* Penguin, Harmondsworth (1954), pp. 114–22.

LEE, S. A. (1975). The 'local area' in the urban context, unpublished paper.

LEE, T. R. (1957). On the relation between the school journey and social and emotional adjustment in rural infant children. *Br. J. educ. Psychol.,* **27,** 101–114.

LEE, T. R. (1962). 'Brennan's law' of shopping behaviour. *Psychol. Rep.,* **11,** 662.

LEE, T. R. (1964). Psychology and living space. *Trans. Bartlett Soc.,* **2,** 9–36. Reprinted in R. M. Downs and D. Stea (1973).

LEE, T. R. (1968). Urban neighbourhood as a socio-spatial schema. *Hum. Relat.,* **21,** 241–67.

LEE, T. R. (1970). Perceived distance as a function of direction in the city. *Envir. Behav.,* **2,** 40–51.

LEE, T. R. (1971). Psychology and architectural determinism. *Architects' J.*, 253–62, 475–83, 651–9.

LENZ-ROMEISS, F. (1973). *The City: New Town or Home Town?*, Pall Mall, London.

LEVINE, G. (1973). From 'know-not-where' to 'nowhere', in H. J. Dyos and M. Wolff, *The Victorian City: Images and Reality,* Routledge & Kegan Paul, London, pp. 495–516.

LEWIN, K. (1935). *A Dynamic Theory of Personality,* McGraw-Hill, New York.

LEWIN, K. (1936). *Principles of Topological Psychology,* McGraw-Hill, New York.

LEWIN, K. (1951). *Field Theory and Social Science,* Harper, New York.

LEWIS, G. M. (1962). Changing emphasis in the description of the natural environment of the Great Plains area. *Trans. Inst. Br. Geogr.,* **30,** 75–90.

LEWIS, J. R. and MELVILLE, B. (1976). The politics of epistemology in regional science. Paper presented to the Ninth Annual Conference of the Regional Science Association (British Section), 12 September 1976, London.

LEY, D. (1974). The city and good and evil: reflections on Christian and Marxist interpretations. *Antipode,* **6,** 66–74.

LORENZ, K. Z. (1966). *On Aggression,* Methuen, London.

LÖSCH, A. (1954). *The Economics of Location,* Yale University Press, New Haven.

LOWENTHAL, D. (1961). Geography, experience and imagination: towards a geographic epistemology. *Ann. Ass. Am. Geogr.,* **51,** 241–60.

LOWENTHAL, D. (1972). Environmental assessment: a comparative analysis of four cities. *Publications in Environmental Perception,* 5, American Geographical Society.

LOWENTHAL, D. (1975). Past time, present place: landscape and memory. *Geogr. Rev.,* **65,** 1–36.

LOWENTHAL, D. and BOWDEN, M. J. (eds) (1976). *Geographies of the Mind,* Oxford University Press, London.

LOWENTHAL, D. and PRINCE, H. C. (1964). The English landscape. *Geogr. Rev.,* **54,** 309–46.

LOWENTHAL, D. and PRINCE, H. C. (1965). English landscape tastes. *Geogr. Rev.,* **55,** 186–222.

LOWENTHAL, D. and RIEL, M. (1972). The nature of perceived

and imagined environments. *Envir. Behav.*, **4**, 189–209.

LOWERY, R. A. (1970). Distance concepts of urban residents. *Envir. Behav.*, **2**, 52–73.

LOWERY, R. A. (1973). A method for analyzing distance concepts of urban residents, in R. M. Downs and D. Stea (eds), *Image and Environment*, Aldine, Chicago, pp. 338–60.

LUKASHOK, A. K. and LYNCH, K. (1956). Some childhood memories of the city. *J. Am. Inst. Plann.*, **22**, 142–52.

LURIE, A. (1966). *The Nowhere City*, Coward-McCann, New York.

LYNCH, K. (1960). *The Image of the City*, M.I.T. Press, Cambridge, Mass.

LYNCH, K. (1972). *What Time is this Place?*, M.I.T. Press, Cambridge, Mass.

LYNCH, K. and RIVKIN, L. G. (1959). A walk around the block. *Landscape*, **8**, 24–34.

McCLENAHAN, B. A. (1945). The communality: the urban substitute for the traditional community. *Sociol. Soc. Res.*, **30**, 264–74.

MacKINDER, H. J. (1935). The progress of geography in the field and in the study during the reign of H. M. King George V. *Geogr. J.*, **86**, 1–12.

McVICAR, J. (1974). *McVicar by Himself*, Hutchinson, London.

MANDEL, E. (1975). *Late Capitalism*, New Left Books, London.

MAURER, R. and BAXTER, J. C. (1972). Images of the neighbourhood and city among black-, Anglo-, and Mexican-American children, *Envir. Behav.*, **4**, 351–88.

MERCER, D. C. and POWELL, J. M. (1972). Phenomenology and related non-positivist view-points in the social sciences. *Monash Publications in Geography*, No. 1, Melbourne.

MERTON, R. K. (1948). The social psychology of housing, in W. Dennis (ed.), *Current Trends in Social Psychology*, University of Pittsburgh Press, Pittsburg, No. 2.

MICHAELSON, W. (1970). *Man and his Environment: A Sociological Approach*, Addison-Wesley, Reading, Mass.

MOORE, G. T. (1973). Developmental differences in environmental cognition, in W. F. E. Preiser (ed.), *Environmental Design Research*, vol. 2, Symposia and Workshops, Dowden, Hutchinson and Ross, Stroudsburg, pp. 232–9.

MOORE, G. T. (1974). The development of environmental knowing: an overview of an interactional-constructivist theory and some

data on within-individual developmental variations, in D. Canter and T. Lee (eds), *Psychology and the Built Environment,* Architectural Press, London, pp. 184–94.
MORRIS, C. (1964). *Signification and Significance,* M.I.T. Press, Cambridge, Mass.
MORRIS, D. (1969). *The Naked Ape,* McGraw-Hill, New York.
MUMFORD, L. (1961). *The City in History,* Seckor & Warburg, London.
NAIRN, I. (1957). *Counter Attack against Subtopia,* Architectural Press, London.
NEISSER, U. (1967). *Cognitive Psychology,* Appleton-Century-Crofts, New York.
NEUTRA, R. (1969). *Survival through Design,* Oxford University Press, New York.
NORBERG-SCHULZ, C. (1965). *Intentions in Architecture,* M.I.T. Press, Cambridge, Mass.
NORBERG-SCHULZ, C. (1971). *Existence, Space and Architecture,* Studio Vista, London.
NORTH OF ENGLAND DEVELOPMENT COUNCIL (1971). *The North in the Sixties,* Newcastle-upon-Tyne.
OLSSON, G. (1970). Explanation, prediction and meaning variance: an assessment of distance interaction models, *Econ. Geogr.,* **46,** 223–33.
OLSSON, G. and GALE, S. (1968). Spatial theory and human behaviour, *Pap. Proc. reg. sci. Ass.,* **21,** 229–42.
OPPENHEIM, R. (1956). Analogy in science, *Am. Psychol.,* **11,** 127–35.
ORLEANS, P. (1973). Differential cognition of urban residents: effects of social scale on mapping, in R. Downs and D. Stea (eds), *Image and Environment,* Aldine, Chicago, pp. 115–30.
ORWELL, G. (1937). *The Road to Wigan Pier,* Gollancz, London.
OSGOOD, C. E., SUCI, G. J. and TANNENBAUM, P. H. (1957). *The Measurement of Meaning,* University of Illinois Press, Urbana.
PACKARD, V. (1957). *The Hidden Persuaders,* Longmans, London.
PAHL, R. E. (1968). Is the mobile society a myth?, *New Soc.,* 11th January, 46–8.
PAHL, R. E. (1975). *Whose City?,* Penguin, Harmondsworth.
PARKINSON, C. N. (1967). Two nations. *The Economist,* 25 March, 116–17.
PARR, A. E. (1965). City and psyche. *Yale Rev.,* **55,** 71–83.

PARSONS, T. (1951). *The Social System,* Routledge and Kegan Paul, London.

PASTERNAK, B. (1958). *Doctor Zhivago,* Collins, London.

PAUL, L. (1964). *The Deployment and Payment of Clergy,* Church Information Office, London.

PETERSON, G. L. (1967). A model for preference: quantitative analysis of the perception of the visual appearance of neighbourhoods. *J. reg. Sci.,* **7,** 19–31.

PETERSON, J. (1916). Illusions of direction orientation. *J. Phil., Psych. Sci. Meth.,* **13,** 225–36.

PIAGET, J. (1968). *Six Psychological Studies,* Vintage, New York.

PIAGET, J. and INHELDER, B. (1967). *The Child's Conception of Space,* Norton, New York.

PLANNING WORKSHOP (1973). Ideologies in planning. *Planning Workshop Paper,* no. 2, Kingston Polytechnic.

POCOCK, D. C. D. (1972*a*). Perspective and urban perception: hypothesis and initial findings. *Archit. Psychol. Newsl.,* **2,** 1–6.

POCOCK, D. C. D. (1972*b*). City of the mind: a review of mental maps of urban areas. *Scott. Geogr. Mag.,* **88,** 115–24.

POCOCK, D. C. D. (1973). Environmental perception: process and product. *Tijdschr. econ. soc. Geogr.,* **64,** 251–7.

POCOCK, D. C. D. (1975). Durham: images of a cathedral city. *Occasional Publications,* Department of Geography, University of Durham, p. 6.

POCOCK, D. C. D. (1976*a*). A comment on images derived from invitation-to-map exercises, *Prof. Geogr.,* **28,** 148–52.

POCOCK, D. C. D. (1976*b*). Some characteristics of mental maps: an empirical study. *Trans. Inst. Br. Geogr.,* **1,** (new series), 493–512.

POPPER, K. R. (1972). *Objective Knowledge: An Evolutionary Approach,* Clarendon, Oxford.

PORTEOUS, J. D. (1971). Design with people: the quality of the urban environment. *Envir. Behav.,* **3,** 155–78.

POULANTZAS, N. (1970). The problem of the Capitalist State, in R. Blackburn (ed.), *Ideology and Social Science,* Fontana, London, pp. 238–53.

PRAED, L. (1863). *History of the Rise and Progress of Middlesbrough,* Middlesbrough.

PRED, A. (1967). Behaviour and location: part I. *Lund Studies in Geography,* Series B, **27,** Lund, Gleerup.

PRIESTLEY, J. B. (1934). *English Journey,* Heinemann, London.

PRINCE, H. (1973). Reality stranger than fiction. *Bloomsbury Geogr.*, **6,** 2–22.

PROSHANSKY, H. M. (1972). Methodology in environmental psychology: problems and issues. *Hum. Fact.*, **14,** 451–60.

RABAN, J. (1974). *Soft City,* Hamilton, London.

RAPOPORT, AMOS (1969). Some aspects of the organisation of urban space, in G. J. Coates and K. M. Moffet (eds), *Response to Environment,* North Carolina State University Press, Raleigh, pp. 122–39.

RAPOPORT, AMOS (1972). Australian aborigines and the defintion of place, in W. J. Mitchel (ed), *Environmental Design Research 3,* vol. 1, Dowden, Hutchinson & Ross, Stroudsburg, sections 3–3–1 to 14.

RAPOPORT, A. and KANTOR, A. (1967). Complexity and ambiguity in environmental design. *Am. Inst. Plann.*, **30,** 210–21.

RAPOPORT, ANATOL (1974). *Conflict in Man-Made Environment,* Penguin, Harmondsworth.

RAVENSTEIN, E. G. (1885). The laws of migration. *J. R. stat. Soc.*, **48,** 52.

REILLY, W. J. (1931). *The Law of Retail Gravitation,* Knickerbocker Press, New York.

RELPH, E. (1970). An enquiry into the relations between phenomenology and geography. *Can. Geogr.*, **14,** 193–209.

RIESER, R. L. (1972). Urban spatial images: an appraisal of the choice of respondents and measurement situation. *Discussion Papers in Geography,* no 42, Graduate School of Geography, London School of Economics, London.

ROZELLE, R. M. and BAXTER, J. C. (1972). Meaning and value in conceptualising the city. *J. Am. Inst. Plann.*, **38,** 116–22.

RUDOFSKY, B. (1969). *Streets for People: A Primer for Americans,* Doubleday, New York.

RUDOFSKY, B. (1973). *Architecture without Architects,* Academy, London.

SAARINEN, T. F. (1966). Perception of drought hazard on the Great Plains. *Research Paper,* 106, Department of Geography, University of Chicago.

SAARINEN, T. F. (1969). Perception of environment. *Resource Paper,* 5, Association of American Geographers, Commission on College Geography.

SCHAEFER, F. (1953). Exceptionalism in geography: a metho-

dological examination. *Ann. Ass. Am. Geogr.*, **43,** 226–49.
SCHAEFER, K. H. and SCLAR, E. (1975). *Access for All,* Penguin, Harmondsworth.
SCHORSKE, C. (1966). The idea of the city in European thought: Voltaire to Spengler, in O. Handlin and J. Burchard (eds), *The Historian and the City,* M.I.T. Press, Cambridge, Mass.
SEARLES, H. F. (1961). The role of the non-human environment. *Landscape,* **11,** 31–4.
SEWELL, D. (1971). Environmental perceptions and attitudes of engineers and public health officials. *Envir. Behav.,* **3,** 23–59.
SHARP, T. (1938). The North-East: hills and hells, in C. Williams-Ellis (ed.), *Britain and the Beast,* Dent. London, pp. 141–59.
SHARP, T. (1968). *Town and Townscape,* Murray, London.
SIEVERTS, T. (1967). Perceptual images of the city of Berlin, in E. J. Brill (ed.), *Urban Core and Inner City,* University of Leiden, pp. 282–5.
SILK, J. (1971). Search behaviour: general characterisation and review of literature in behavioural sciences. *Geographical Papers,* no. 7, Department of Geography, University of Reading.
SILLITOE, A. (1975). *Mountains and Caverns,* Allen, London.
SIMON, H. A. (1957). *Models of Man: Social and Rational,* Wiley, New York.
SKINNER, B. F. (1953). *Science and Human Behaviour,* Macmillan, London.
SMITH, P. F. (1972). Criteria for development control. *Built Envir.* 633–6.
SMITH, P. F. (1974*a*). Familiarity breeds contentment. *The Planner,* 901–4.
SMITH, P. F. (1974*b*). Human rights in architecture. *The Planner,* 953–5.
SMITH, P. F. (1974*c*). *The Dynamics of Urbanism,* Hutchinson, London.
SMITHSONIAN Institute (1970). *The Fitness of Man's Environment,* Smithsonian Institute Press, Washington.
SOCKETT, A. (ed.) (1889). *Record of Proceedings at Opening of the Middlesbrough Town Hall,* Middlesbrough.
SOMMER, R. (1969). *Personal Space: The Behavioural Basis of Design,* Prentice-Hall, Englewood Cliffs.
SOMMER, R. (1972). *Design Awareness,* Rhinehart, San Francisco.
SONNENFELD, J. (1969). Personality and behaviour in the en-

vironment. *Proc. Ass. Am. Geogr.,* **1,** 136–40.

SOUTH HAMPSHIRE PLAN ADVISORY COMMITTEE (1970). *Urban Form: the Built Environment,* South Hampshire Plan, Study Report C.

SOUTHWORTH, M. (1969). The sonic environment of cities. *Envir. Behav.,* **1**, 49–70.

SOUTHWORTH, M. and SOUTHWORTH, S. (1973). Environmental quality in cities and regions. *Tn. Plann. Rev.,* **44,** 231–53.

SPENCER, D. and LLOYD, J. (1974). The Small Heath schools session: mental maps of routes from home to school. *Working Paper,* 24, Centre for Urban & Regional Studies, University of Birmingham.

STEA, D. (1969*a*). The measurement of mental maps: an experimental model for studying conceptual spaces, in K. R. Cox and R. G. Golledge (eds), Behavioural problems in geography: a symposium. *Northwestern University, Studies in Geography,* **17,** pp. 228–53.

STEA, D. (1969*b*). Environmental perception and cognition: towards a model for mental maps, in G. J. Coates and K. M. Moffett (eds), *Response to Environment,* School of Design, Raleigh, N. C., pp. 63–76.

STEA, D. and BLAUT, J. M. (1973*a*). Notes towards a developmental theory of spatial learning, in R. Downs and D. Stea (eds), *Image and Environment,* Aldine, Chicago, pp. 51–62.

STEA, D. and BLAUT, J. M. (1973*b*). Some preliminary observations on spatial learning in school children, in R. Downs and D. Stea (eds). *Image and Environment,* Aldine, Chicago, pp. 226–34.

STEINITZ, C. (1968). Meaning and congruence of urban form and activity. *Am. Inst. Plann.,* **34,** 233–48.

STEVENS, B. H. (1961). An application of game theory to a problem in locational strategy. *Pap. Proc. reg. Sci. Ass.* **7,** 143–57.

STEWART, J. Q. (1950). The development of social physics. *Am. J. Phys.,* **18,** 239–53.

STRANGE, G. R. (1968). The Victorian city and the frightened poets. *Vict. Stud.,* **11,** 627–40.

STRANGE, G. R. (1973). The frightened poets, in H. J. Dyos and M. Wolff, *The Victorian City: Images and Reality,* Routledge & Kegan Paul, London, pp. 475–94.

STRAUSS, A. (1968). *The American City: A Sourcebook of Urban Imagery,* Aldine, Chicago.

STRINGER, P. (1975). Understanding the city, in D. Canter (ed.), *Environmental Interaction,* Surrey University Press, pp. 253–80.

SUMMERSON, J. (1964). *The Classical Language of Architecture,* Methuen, London.

THIEL, P. (1962). A sequence-experience notion for architecture and urban spaces. *Tn. Plann. Rev.,* **33,** 33–52.

THOMAS, D. (1967). *The Visible Persuaders,* Hutchinson, London.

THOMAS, R. and CRESSWELL, P. (1973). The new town idea. *Urban Development,* Unit 26, The Open University.

THOMPSON, D. L. (1963). New concept: subjective distance. *J. Retail.,* **39,** pp. 1–6, reprinted in P. Ambrose (1969), *Analytical Human Geography,* Longmans, London.

THORNS, D. C. (1972). *Suburbia,* MacGibbon and Kee, London.

TOFFLER, A. (1970). *Future Shock,* Bodley Head, London.

TOLMAN, E. C. (1932). *Purposive Behaviour in Animals and Man,* Appleton-Century-Crofts, New York.

TOLMAN, E. C. (1948). Cognitive maps in rats and men. *Psychol. Rev.,* **55,** 189–208.

TOLMAN, E. C. (1952). A cognition – motivation model. *Psychol. Rev.,* **59,** 389–400.

TOLMAN, E. C. (1963). Principles of purposive behaviour, in S. Koch (ed.), *Psychology: Study of a Science,* vol. 5, McGraw-Hill, New York.

TORGERSON, W. S. (1958). *Theory and Methods of Scaling,* J. Wiley, New York.

TOWNROE, P. (1974). Industrial location search behaviour and regional development, in J. Rees and P. Newby (eds), Behavioural perspectives in geography, *Middlesex Polytechnic Monographs in Geography,* no. 1, pp. 45–58.

TOWNSEND, A. R. and TAYLOR, C.C. (1975). Regional culture and identity in industrialised societies: the case of North-East England. *Reg. Stud.,* **9,** 379–93.

TROWBRIDGE, C. C. (1912). On fundamental methods of orientation and imaginary maps. *Science, N.Y.,* **38,** 888–97.

TROY, P. N. (1971). *Environmental Quality in Four Sydney Suburban Areas,* Social Sciences Urban Research Unit, Australian National University, Canberra.

TUAN, Y. F. (1971*a*). Geography, phenomenology and the study of human nature. *Can. Geogr.,* **15,** 181–92.

TUAN, Y. F. (1971*b*). Man and nature. Association of American Geographers, *Resource Paper,* **10**, Commission on College Geography.

TUAN, Y. F. (1972). Environmental psychology: a review. *Geogr. Rev.* **62,** 245–51.

TUAN, Y. F. (1973). Ambiguity in attitudes towards environment, *Ann. Ass. Ann. Geogr.,* **63,** 411–23.

TUAN, Y. F. (1974*a*). *Topophilia,* Prentice-Hall, New Jersey.

TUAN, Y. F. (1974*b*). Space and place: humanistic perspective. *Progr. Geogr.,* **6,** 211–52.

TUAN, Y. F. (1975). Images and mental maps. *Ann. Ass. Am. Geogr.,* **65,** 205–13.

TUAN, Y. F. (1976). Geopiety: a theme in man's attachment to nature and to place, in D. Lowenthal and M. J. Bowden (eds), *Geographies of the Mind,* Oxford University Press, London, pp. 11–39.

VENTURI, R., BROWN, D. S. and IZENOUR, S. (1973). Learning from Las Vegas, in W. H. Ittelson (ed.), *Environment and Cognition,* Seminar Press, New York, pp. 99–112.

VERNON, M. D. (1962). *The Psychology of Perception,* Penguin, Harmondsworth.

WALMSLEY, D. J. (1974). Positivism and phenomenology in human geography. *Can. Geogr,* **18,** 95–107.

WARR, P. B. and KNAPPER, C. (1968). *The Perception of People and Events,* Wiley, London.

WATSON, J. B. (1919). *Psychology from the Standpoint of a Behaviourist,* Lippincott, Philadelphia.

WATSON, J. W. (1969). The role of illusion in North American geography. *Can. Geogr.* **13,** 10–27.

WATSON, J. W. (1972). Mental distance in geography: its identification and representation. Paper read at I.G.U. Symposium in Montreal.

WEATHERBEE, M. (1886). Europe on nothing-certain a year. *Century ill. Mag.,* **32,** pp. 937–41.

WEBBER, M. (1964*a*). The urban place and the non-place urban realm, in M. Webber (ed.), *Explorations in Urban Structure,* University of Pennsylvania Press, Pittsburgh.

WEBBER, M. (1964*b*). Culture, territoriality and the elastic mile. Pap. Proc. Reg. Sc. Ass., **13,** pp. 59–70.

WERNER, H. (1957). The concept of development from a comparative and organismic point of view, in D. B. Harris (ed.), *The Concept of Development, University of Minnesota Press, Minneapolis,* pp. 125–48.

WERTHEIMER, M. (1938). Laws of organisation in perceptual forms, in W. D. Ellis (ed.), *A Source Book of Gestalt Psychology,* Routledge & Kegan Paul, London.

WHEATLEY, P. (1971). *The Pivot of Four Quarters,* University of Edinburgh Press, Edinburgh.

WILKINSON, E. C. (1939). *The Town that was Murdered,* Gollancz, London.

WILLIAMS, R. (1973). *The Country and the City,* Chatto & Windus, London.

WILLIAMS, S. H. (1954). 'Urban aesthetics' *Tn. Plann. Rev.,* **25,** 95–113.

WILSON, A. G. (1971). A family of spatial interaction models and associated developments. *Envir. Plann.,* **3,** 1–32.

WILSON, A. G. (1974). *Urban and Regional Models in Geography and Planning,* Wiley, London.

WILSON, R. L. (1962). Livability of the city: attitudes and urban development, in F. S. Chapin and S. F. Weiss, *Urban Growth Dynamics in a Regional Cluster of Cities,* Wiley, New York, pp. 359–99.

WOHL, A. S. (1973). Unfit for human habitation, in H. J. Dyos and M. Wolff, *The Victorian City: Images and Reality,* Routledge & Kegan Paul, London, pp. 603–24.

WOLPERT, J. (1963). The decision process in a spatial context. *Ann. Ass. Am. Geogr.,* **54,** 537–58.

WOOD, W. (1970). Perception studies in geography. *Trans. Inst. Br. Geogr.,* **50,** 129–41.

WURMAN, R. S. (1971). Making the city observable. *Design Q.,* **80,** 1–96.

YLIVSAKER, P. (1971). *Old Cities and New Towns,* Alvin Schwarz, London.

YOUNG, G. (1973). *Tourism – Blessing or Blight?,* Penguin, Harmondsworth.

Author Index

Place Index

Subject Index